MINI
CRETE

ROUGH GUIDES

How to download your Free eBook

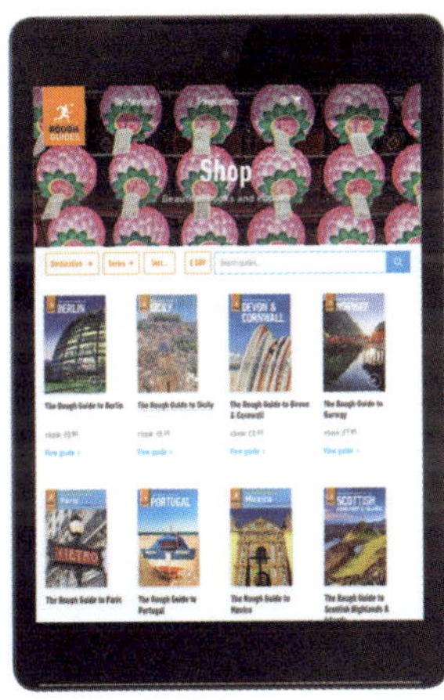

1. Visit **www.roughguides.com/free-ebook** or scan the **QR code** opposite

2. Enter the code **crete086**

3. Follow the simple step-by-step instructions

For troubleshooting contact: mail@roughguides.com

Samsonite

Contents

Introduction

Crete: the name invokes a variety of images. Ancient sites to explore; commercial towns bustling with noise and traffic; millions of olive trees blanketing the countryside; raucous resorts with neon-lit bars and loud music; a romantic meal for two overlooking a small fishing port; mountains and gorges to trek through; a sunlounger on a beach, among hundreds of others, similarly soaking up the rays; fifteen hours of sunshine a day in summer; three feet of snow in the mountains in winter. The island has something for everyone, and its sheer variety satisfies even the most jaded and cynical traveller.

The 'Great Island'

Crete sits in the eastern Mediterranean Sea, just 110 nautical miles north of the African coast and an even shorter sea-crossing from Anatolia. Its strategic position, at the crossroads of trade north from Egypt, west from Rome and east from the Middle East, made it valuable territory from the earliest days of trade and power politics.

Covering an area of 8,300 sq km (3,200 sq miles), Crete is sometimes called Megalónissos, or 'Great Island'. Visually, it is stunning, with three dramatic mountain ranges over 2,000m (6,500ft) high that seem to anchor the island in the sea. Water has cut vertiginous gorges through the mountains and opened huge cave systems through their hearts. These caves were places of great religious significance to the ancient Cretans; in some cases they were thought to be the

NOTES

Crete is divided into four administrative districts (*periféries* in Greek), mostly named after their governing cities: Iráklio, the most populous, with the island's capital; Haniá; Lasíthi (based in Ágios Nikólaos); and Réthymno. Within each you'll find the many smaller towns and villages as mentioned throughout this guide.

birthplaces of Greek gods. Over the centuries, these caverns provided protection for pirates, vagabonds and freedom fighters. The mountains were never fully conquered, even during World War II – their furthest valleys were too remote, their slopes too steep. Today, their peaks are the domain of numerous birds of prey, including eagles, hawks and vultures.

Natural landscape

Fertile plateaus and lowlands have been settled and farmed since Neolithic times; abundant fresh spring water from the surrounding peaks helped ensure a rich harvest. Around the coastline – especially in the north – long sandy stretches have attracted visitors since the 1960s, with the advent of package tours, but variety exists here too, with several different coastal environments; rocky coves, rugged headlands and marshy wetlands.

The fruitful year

Despite its southerly latitude, seasons remain distinct on Crete. Springtime sees the hills awash with flowers and wheat crops ripening in the warming sun, goat kids are born and the flocks make the most of fresh pastures. As summer starts, cereals are harvested and the land takes on an ochre hue. Birdsong gives way to the sound of cicadas, and the smell of honeysuckle rises in the evening air. Midsummer sees Cretans seeking shade to escape the heat,

WHEN TO GO

Crete is a year-round destination, but each season offers a distinct experience.

High season (June–August) is the hottest, busiest, and most expensive time to visit. Expect packed beaches, bustling old towns, and temperatures soaring to the mid-30s°C. It's great for sun-seekers and nightlife, but don't expect solitude – the island is at full capacity with tourists.

Shoulder season (March–May and September–November) offers warm, pleasant days averaging 24°C, ideal for sightseeing and beach time without the crowds. Spring brings wildflowers and Easter festivities, while autumn has slightly warmer seas and a relaxed vibe. Late April to June and September to October are particularly appealing for their mild weather and fewer tourists.

Low season (December–February) sees the fewest visitors. The weather can be cold and wet, especially inland, with temperatures occasionally dropping to 0°C. Many tourist businesses shut down, but larger towns like Iráklio and Haniá stay lively. It's not beach weather, but it's ideal for cultural experiences and escaping the crowds – just bring warm clothing.

For the best mix of comfort, culture, and calm, aim for the shoulder months.

while visitors head out in droves to work on their tans. The clanging of livestock bells can be heard across the countryside as flocks desperately search for sustenance in the parched hills.

Autumn brings a cooling of the temperature, yet a warming of the landscape as colours mellow in the lower arc of the late season sun. Stucco on buildings takes on a rosy hue, the grapes swell to tempting perfection and citrus fruits begin their transition from green to orange. All too soon, winter brings a blanket of snow to the mountains; ordinarily dry ravines and pastures swell with rain run-off, wood smoke fills the air, and the old folk retreat to their warm hearths.

The olive harvest is the main focal point of the year. This crop reigns supreme and millions of trees blanket hillside slopes and coastal plains, a symbol of man's reliance on the earth. It has sustained Cretans for too long to be treated with disdain.

The cradle of Europe

The footsteps of history can be seen on every dusty path and urban street. Crete was the cradle of European civilisation, and the Minoans – believed to be mythological until evidence of their existence was confirmed early in the twentieth century – travelled far and wide across the eastern Mediterranean for trade.

A prodigious collection of artefacts now displayed in museums across the island shows them to be the first Indigenous European culture whose lives were graced by art, sports and the pursuit of pleasure. The Minoan civilisation suffered a sudden and terminal collapse around 1450BC for reasons that have not been fully established.

Tour group visiting Knossos Palace

A devastating natural disaster was initially thought to be the cause, but archeological theories now consider either invasion by a warring people or internal revolt to be the most likely scenarios. Whatever the case, the catastrophe heralded the start of thousands of years of invasion and subjection for

A mountain village scene

the Cretans: Mycenaeans, Dorians, Athenians, Macedonians, Romans, Byzantines, Arabs, Venetians and Ottomans all came to take control. Evidence of their presence abounds in the commanding fortresses, protective harbours, fine mansions, narrow winding alleys, elegant minarets and ornate fountains of the towns. In 1913, Crete finally achieved a long-awaited *énosis* (union) with Orthodox Christian Greece.

Freedom or death

Cretans did not take kindly to their native land being usurped and, particularly in the years of Turkish rule, they gained a reputation as formidable and tenacious fighters who struck with speed, then retreated to mountain strongholds to outwit their enemies.

They reverted back to the same lifestyle during World War II when Crete was captured by German forces, mounting a successful guerrilla resistance and living up to the old rallying cry – 'freedom or death'.

Invaders would occupy the cities, but they could never manage to tame the people of the countryside. For centuries, unbowed Cretans lived simple lives in harmony with the land; tending their flocks, growing fruit and vegetables, and harvesting the sea. Clothes and carpets were made of wool, leather was used to make boots and saddles, wood was used for bowls and utensils, and grass and straw woven into basketry. Seasonal surpluses were stored to provide sustenance for the long winters that often isolated mountain villages. The people put their trust in God, as the many Orthodox churches across the island attest, praying for self-determination and for their menfolk hiding out in the hills.

Enduring traditions

Although peace now reigns, a glance around communities in the Cretan heartland still suggests that little has changed. Whitewashed villages dot the landscape, each house with its own smallholding.

WHAT'S NEW

Crete has seen a vibrant wave of new openings and cultural developments in recent years. Here's what's fresh and upcoming:

Ombros-Gialos Diving Park (Haniá) – Open since summer 2025, this 60,000m² underwater park has artificial reefs and two sunken warships, offering three diving routes for all skill levels (https://kefidivers.com/post/discover-the-new-diving-park-in-apokoronas-crete).

Asteroscholeio at Skinakas Observatory (Anogeia) Set to debut in 2025, this €1 million educational centre will enhance astrotourism with a 360m² facility, including an 85-seat hall for public astronomy events (skinakas.physics.uoc.gr/en/home).

Museum of Cretan Folklore (Daphnes, Iráklio periféreia) – Opened in 2024 and half an hour drive inland from Iráklio, this museum showcases rare weavings and icons within the Varoucha Estate, offering insights into Crete's rich cultural heritage.

Papoura Hill Minoan Site (Kastelli) – Discovered in June 2024, this four-thousand-year-old circular structure is a significant archaeological find, now being preserved amidst airport construction.

Red Jane Bakery (Haniá) (https://instagram.com/redjaneproject) Opened in 2023 in a repurposed abandoned interwar factory from the 1930s, this artisanal bakery is part of Chania's culinary renaissance offering sourdough delights in a unique setting.

The traditional diet – greens, olive oil, wild herbs, honey, yoghurt and a little lamb or goat meat – still sustains these rural people, and it has been scientifically proven to be one of the healthiest in the world. Though traditions are dying, some older men still stride out in black breeches, leather boots and crocheted headbands worn by

SUSTAINABLE TRAVEL

Visitors to Crete can travel responsibly by making eco-conscious choices that both reduce their environmental impact and support the local community. Walk around cities such as Iráklio, Réthymno or Haniá or join cycling tours offered in areas like Réthymno and Hersonissos, where designated cycling lanes exist. Several companies offer e-bike tours in Crete, catering to different interests and fitness levels. Popular options include tours focused on culture, food, and nature, as well as guided tours with experienced guides: cyclingcreta.gr/e-bike-tours-crete offers guided e-bike tours exploring various areas, including canyons, villages, and landscapes. In Iráklio, the city's electric bus service provides a green alternative to driving.

For dining, head to *Koukouvaya*, a 13-min drive east from Haniá Old Town, or *Vegera* in Zaros village, one hour inland from Iráklio, both offer exceptional plant-based dishes made with local produce, the latter also running traditional cookery classes. Supporting small, family-run tavernas in inland villages also keeps revenue from tourism within the community.

Explore lesser-visited areas like the Amári Valley (see page 80) or the verdant region of Hóra Sfakíon (see page 82). These spots offer scenic hiking trails without the crowds. Nature lovers should consider visiting the *Samariá Gorge National Park* (see page 91) or *Váï* (see page 71), both of which protect endemic flora and fauna.

Avoid overcrowded beaches like Elafónisos during peak season (see page 89), opting for quieter stretches such as Xérokambos (see page 73) or a day trip to Hrissí (Gaïdouro) islet from Ierápetra (see page 74), where dunes and juniper trees provide a more serene setting. Respect local habitats and leave no trace.

previous generations while widows in black sit quietly knitting in their doorways and goats graze slopes that no farmer could use.

If a Cretan's hatred of his enemy is legendary, it has always been surpassed by, in contrast, the generosity expressed to his friends – and by extension to strangers (*xénos* is the Greek word for both stranger and friend). A door is always open to a passing traveller. Today, admiring an orchard or a ripening vineyard even in rudimentary Greek will result in an armful of fruit to take with you on your journey – just a small example of how tradition carries on through the generations. And how do today's Cretans find their pleasure? Poetry, literature, music and dance; traditional forms of all these arts are still alive and well here.

The observatory on Mt Psiloritis

Crete is also a modern and urbanised island. Since the 1980s, many remote interior villages have all but emptied in favour of the largest coastal towns which are continuously expanding. Young Cretans are just as interested in fashion, higher education and music as their peninsular-Greek cousins. They aim to find jobs with excitement, a secure future and ready cash to spend – something many feel a rural way of life cannot offer them. Even during ongoing economic downturn, the three largest north-coast Cretan towns of Iráklio, Réthymno and Haniá have active commercial sectors and vibrant intellectual scenes, aspects of the island that surprise many visitors.

10 Things not to miss

1

2

3

4

5

6

1 **ÁGIOS NIKÓLAOS**
The prettiest town in the east of the island is a popular resort that preserves its Cretan charm. See page 62.

2 **ARCHAEOLOGICAL MUSEUM OF IRÁKLIO**
Packed with priceless Minoan finds. See page 42.

3 **SAMARIÁ GORGE**
The longest gorge in Europe is a strenuous but exhilarating trek. See page 91.

4 **MONÍ ARKADÍOU**
A shrine to the Cretan struggle for independence. See page 79.

5 **HANIÁ**
The minaret-style lighthouse and scenic harbour are amongst many of Haniá's highlights. See page 85.

6 **MONÍ TOPLOÚ**
A peaceful place with a bloody history. See page 70.

7 **GORTYS**
The capital of Crete in Roman and Byzantine times. See page 52.

8 **KNOSSOS**
Its Minoan palace, with superb frescoes, is Crete's most visited attraction. See page 47.

9 **LASÍTHI PLATEAU**
Home to rural life and ancient windmills. See page 66.

10 **RÉTHYMNO**
Réthymno's attractive Venetian harbour is lined with dozens of fish restaurants. See page 75.

A perfect tour of Crete

DAY 1

Iráklio Old Town. Start with coffee and *bougatsa* at *Kirkor* in Liontaria Square. Visit the Iráklio Archaeological Museum for Minoan culture (https://heraklionmuseum.gr/en). See the Venetian walls and Morosini Fountain, then lunch at *Paradosiako.* Cool off at Ammoudara Beach (11 minutes by car). For sunset, head to the Koules fortress, then dine at *Peskesi* (see page 125).

DAY 2

Hills around Archanes. Drive 30 minutes inland to Archanes. Visit its small museum of Minoan treasures then lunch at shady *Taverna Istorikón*. Spend the afternoon wine-tasting at Lyrarakis (https://lyrarakis.com/en), then return via the Minoan Palace of Knossos (knossos-palace.gr). Wrap up with seafood at *Ippokambos*, overlooking the harbour.

DAY 3

West to Réthymno. Take a direct bus (1hr 15mins) or drive (1hr) via Moní Arkadíou (arkadimonastery.gr). Start at the Fortezza (visit-rethymno.gr/rethymno), then do coffee at Rimondi Fountain's *Cafe Galero*. After exploring the Old Town, lunch at *Raki Ba Raki*, then swim at Réthymno Beach. Later, dine harbourside at *Prima Plora* (https://primaplora.gr).

DAY 4

Lake Kourná and Rural Apokoronou. En route to Haniá, stop 30-mins inland at Lake Kourná, Crete's only freshwater lake for coffee or a pedalo. Continue to Gavalochori and visit the brilliant Folklore Museum located in a traditional house painted green in the square. In Haniá, enjoy dinner at *Tamam* in a former hamam.

DAY 5

Haniá Town. Begin with coffee from any spot overlooking the Venetian lighthouse. Visit the Maritime Museum of Crete, housed in a beautiful building by the entrance to Firka Fortress. Lunch at *To Maridaki*, then shop in the Splantzia district and Agora for olives and Cretan honey. Finish with dinner by the water.

DAY 6

Sea and serenity. Spend the morning at Plataniás Beach (20-mins by car west). On the way back, detour to the village of Vouves, home to the oldest olive tree on the island (thought to be over four thousand years old). Visit the small Olive Museum next door (free), then lunch at *Eleasthea* (https://eleasthea.gr) in the village before returning to Haniá for an afternoon at Al Hammam Traditional Baths. Afterwards, enjoy dinner at *Oinoa Wine Restaurant*.

DAY 7

Wind-down. Back in Iráklio, explore the Historical Museum. Snack at Armenian-run *Kirkor* which serves great *bougátsa* (custard pastry) and *tyrópittes* (cheese pies), then toast your trip goodbye with sunset drinks at *The Bitters Bar.*

Crete for foodies

8AM

Coffee and kalitsounia in Haniá Old Town. Set yourself up for the day at *Ntourountous Bakery & Coffee Shop*, about an 8-min walk from Haniá Old Town's, known for its excellent coffee brews and *kalitsounia* (sweet or savoury Cretan cheese or herb pastries, a popular and beloved local staple). Their debut family bakery in the village of Sfakia spread in popularity across the island. Alternatively, the *Red Jane Bakery* is housed in a unique setting – a previously abandoned 1930s interwar building and is popular for its sourdough breads and pastries.

9AM

Haniá Central Market (Agora). A five-minute stroll from both *Ntourountous* and *Red Jane* brings you to the one-hundred-year-old Central Market. Locals shop for *dakos* rusks, herbs, honey, olives, and cheeses like *graviera*. Sample as you wander through.

10:30AM

Olive oil and cheese tasting. Drive 35 minutes to *Melissakis Olive Mill* near Vamos village (https://melissakis.gr). Join a guided tasting and learn the difference between early harvest and late press oils. Continue with a cheese tasting at *Vamos Cheese Co-op* (vamosvillage.gr/activities/visit-the-local-producers), including *myzithra* and *anthotyros* local varieties, and where you'll have the opportunity to visit local producers during a fuller tour starting at 10am daily except Sunday from Vamos Tourist Office (min. 6 people; €75 pp), so if you opt for this, leave earlier from Haniá.

12:30PM

Farm-to-table cooking. Join a hands-on Cretan traditional cooking session in 'Fabrica', an old olive press dating from 1846 with Venetian arches and large millstones in the heart of Vamos (https://vamosvillage.gr/activities/cooking-lessons). You'll prepare a full Cretan lunch with fresh, local ingredients: ntakos, stuffed vine leaves (dolmadakia), and slow-cooked lamb with artichokes. Wash it down with local wine in the garden.

3:45PM

Digestive walk and relax. A thirty-minute drive inland takes you to Lake Kourná (see page 83). Wander the natural shores and have a coffee or juice at *Ambrosia* with its balconied amphitheatrical views of the lake. The food is excellent here and it closes late, and with its gorgeous views, you may be tempted to linger.

6PM

An organic end to the day. Drive 35 minutes to Rethymno for an early evening stroll along the harbour front. At *Prima Plora*, enjoy an organic meal overlooking the Fortress. Choose from a simple *Dakos* salad (barley rusk, tomato and *myzithra* soft cheese) to richer dishes such as octopus with fava or cuttlefish ink risotto – it's the perfect way to round off your day.

Beach hopping in Crete

8AM

Coffee in Kissamos. Begin your sun-filled day of beach hopping of Crete's pink-sand lagoons, wild peninsulas and crystal-clear coves at *Breeze*, a relaxed spot along Kissamos seafront. It's perfect for a Greek coffee or smoothie alongside a hearty breakfast of an omelette or waffles. Bask in the setting of the Gulf of Kissamos from a pavement table or enjoy loftier views from the rooftop.

9:30AM

Head to Balos Lagoon by Boat. From Kissamos, drive ten minutes to its small port and catch the seasonal boat trip (check it's running at the time of your visit) to *Balos Lagoon* – Crete's famed turquoise stretch of coastline where powdery white sand meets shallow, cerulean waters. Surrounded by the wild Gramvousa Peninsula, it's ideal for paddling, wading and soaking up the gorgeous views (https://cretandailycruises.com/explorecruises/gramvousabalos.en.html; charge).

3PM

Lunch with a Sea View. After returning from your Balos Lagoon boat trip (10:00am–2:00pm), drive just over an hour south to Elafonissi Beach. Before sinking into its famous pink sands, enjoy a relaxed late lunch at family-run, upmarket *Taverna Kalomirakis* (https://elafonisi-resort.com/restaurant), which has superb sea views and a lovely, covered terrace. It also offers accommodation so you could always stay the night if you don't want to rush back home but it's advisable to book ahead.

4PM

Discover the Pink Sands of Elafonissi Beach. Remote Elafonissi beach in the southwest of the island is famous for its powdery, blush-coloured sand (formed by crushed seashells). Its shallow turquoise waters are perfect for those travelling with little ones. Wade through the warm lagoon to the small islet, a Natura 2000 protected area rich in rare flora and sand dunes. The atmosphere here feels almost Caribbean, yet it is still unmistakably Cretan.

6PM

Sunset Swim at Falassarna. Drive back north for just over an hour to reach Falassarna Beach in time for sunset. This expansive, west-facing beach is ideal for a final dip in the water or simply lounging with a drink from the beach bar. The sun melts into the sea in a blaze of orange and pink, this is one of the island's most photogenic spots.

8:15PM

Dinner. Return to Kissamos for dinner (25 minutes) or head on to Chania (1hr15min) reflecting on Crete's striking coastlines and beachside bliss.

History

Crete's history is bound up with its strategic position between Western Europe, the Middle East and North Africa. In good times, this brought trade, creative ideas and prosperity; in bad times, invasion, oppression and disease. Many fascinating legacies around the island attest to the complicated web that time has spun here.

The earliest human remains found on Crete date back to the seventh millennium BC. These first inhabitants were Neolithic hunter-gatherers who came from Asia Minor. They developed into farmers, with settlements on the fertile Messará Plain. It was an influx of new, more skilled settlers shortly after 3000BC that ushered in the Minoan era, the first major civilisation to arise on European soil.

Minoan Crete

A great ancient Cretan civilisation was for many years believed to be merely the stuff of mythology until Sir Arthur Evans, its principal advocate, made reality out of folklore and myth (see page 47). At its zenith, Minoan Crete's population numbered more than two million with one hundred thousand people living in the capital, Knossos. These early Bronze Age settlements were built without fortifications and comprised vast numbers of dwellings. The first palatial structures at Knossos, Phaestos (modern Festós) and Malia, were erected between 2000–1900BC, but were destroyed by an earthquake around 1700BC. The remains today are their even bigger and more splendid replacements. This golden age of Minoan society – known as the Neo-Palatial era – lasted about 250 years.

The Minoans

Ruled by a priest-king, who presided over religious and economic affairs, it is unclear whether one reigned over the entire island or if each palace settlement had its own regional king. His people worshipped the Mother Goddess, and divine power was symbolised

A 3,500-year-old fresco of three Minoan women in Knossos

by the bull, the focus of ornate and elaborate rituals. One sacred symbol, at odds with their peaceful lifestyle, is the *labrys* (double-headed axe). Its image has been found on various artefacts.

The Minoans developed an alphabet and printing method, along with sophisticated plumbing and water-delivery systems. Women enjoyed high status, playing an active part in palace life, and the whole population enjoyed athletic contests, games and recreational activities. Above all, they excelled in the visual arts. Wherever there was a blank 'canvas' there was imagery: decorative entrances, walls, floors and pottery. Many breathtaking examples can be seen in the Archaeological Museum in Iráklio (see page 42). Gold and precious stones were fashioned into beautiful jewellery, indicating a high quality of life fuelled by trade. Cretans exhibited their skills with paint, clay, copper and bronze, but also with imported raw materials – lapis lazuli from Afghanistan, ivory from Syria, gold, silver and black obsidian from Anatolia. Copper and bronze were worked and re-exported, along with olive oil, honey and wine.

The Minoans developed into one of the great naval powers of the Mediterranean, with wood from the island's vast juniper and cypress forests providing ample material for boats. However, they concentrated their power more on commercial than military gain, showing a taste for the good life over hunger for an empire.

This great civilisation came to a sudden, catastrophic end in around 1450BC. The exact cause remains unknown, but all the palaces were destroyed at the same time. Charred remains at Knossos and ash at Zakros suggest a great conflagration. A leading theory was that natural disaster struck the island in the wake of the volcanic explosion on Thíra (Santoríni), due north of Crete, bringing tidal waves, earthquakes and fire storms. But Thíra exploded in about 1500BC, a half-century before the Cretan destruction. More recent research has favoured another hypothesis – that an attack by invaders or domestic rebel forces may have brought about its demise.

Dorians and Romans

After the disaster, Mycenaean Greeks from the Peloponnese moved in to control what remained of the Minoan settlements – they may even have precipitated the destruction. Around 1200BC, Dorian

THE ROMAN CONQUEST

It took the Romans three years of brutal fighting to conquer Crete in 67BC, and they did so only by playing the rival city-states against one another. Crete remained a province of the Roman Empire until AD395, with Gortys as its capital. The Romans brought a certain order to the island, putting an end to internal struggles, building new roads, ports and aqueducts, and introducing systems of domestic plumbing and central heating akin to those in use today.

invaders from the Balkans drove south through the Greek mainland, across the Aegean and into Crete. Many coastal dwellers migrated to mountain settlements; others overseas. Crete was not directly involved in Greece's Persian and Peloponnesian Wars but it was a valuable source of brave mercenaries.

Lató was the dominant city during the Dorian occupation

While mainland Greece was reaching its zenith during the Classical Age (480–338BC), Crete remained a backwater of warring city-states, of which Gortys (modern Górtyna) was the most powerful. Nevertheless, enlightened Athenians acknowledged Crete as a source of culture, and its caves and shrines were centres of pilgrimage. The island's most significant remnant from this period is the law code of Gortys (see page 52), which reveals a hierarchical society ruled by an aristocratic class.

Early Christians

The apostle Paul arrived in AD60–61, and by AD64 had charged his disciple Titus to convert the islanders to Christianity. Titus had a hard time combating local pagan beliefs, but died peacefully in AD107, as bishop of Gortys, and Titus became Crete's patron saint. The Greek Orthodox Church has always played a special role on Crete, it funded schools teaching Greek language and tradition and it was the focus of unity and resistance to oppression.

When Roman power split in two, the eastern Byzantine Empire inherited the island. Attacks by pirates and Islamic forces brought terror to the people, but Cretans remained loyal to the Orthodox Church throughout the occupation by Andalucian pirates in AD824 to 961. The island was recaptured after a terrible siege of Iráklio by Byzantine commander (and subsequently emperor) Nikeforos Phokas, during which he catapulted the heads of dead Arabs into the city to dishearten surviving defenders.

Venetian days

After Byzantium fell to the Crusaders in 1204, Crete was given to their leader, Boniface of Montferrat, who immediately sold it to Venice for 1,000 silver marks, ushering in a new era. Crete prospered greatly under the 465 years of Venetian occupation (1204–1669), although during the first century there were repeated revolts by both Venetian colonists and displaced Byzantine aristocracy. As a source of shipbuilding timber in a key location, the island was a linchpin in the far-flung commercial empire, and became the Republic's first formally constituted overseas colony.

The complex legal code of Gortys was carved in stone

The arts flourished during the fifteenth and sixteenth

THE CRETAN RENAISSANCE

After the fall of Constantinople in 1453, Crete became a haven for artists and theologians fleeing the Ottomans. A religious college for the study of painting, theology and the humanities was established at the Church of Agía Ekateríni in Iráklio (see page 42), which became the centre of the Cretan Renaissance during the sixteenth and seventeenth centuries. El Greco is said to have studied here, along with his contemporary Mihaïl Damaskinos, and Vitsentzos Kornaros, the author of the epic poem *Erotokritos*.

Cretan artists excelled at icon painting, blending traditional Byzantine style with influences from Renaissance Italy. Their work was in demand throughout the Western world. Damaskinos, who worked in Venice from 1577 to 1582, was the master of this art. His use of colour and perspective brought a depth to the icon tradition that was widely imitated.

centuries, a period known as the Cretan Renaissance. Numerous new monasteries and churches were built and icon-painting attained new heights after an influx of artists from Byzantium after 1453, who founded important schools of art.

The great literary figure of the time, Vitsentzos Kornaros (1553–1613), wrote a romantic epic poem in Cretan dialect, the *Erotokritos*. Even if most villagers can no longer recite it by heart, it is still acclaimed among the literati of Crete.

The battle for Crete

In the eastern Mediterranean, Christian forces were in retreat as a new Muslim power began to expand. The Ottoman Turks pushed Venetian and Genoese forces out of Asia Minor and the Greek mainland, and then from most islands of the Aegean. Eventually it would be Crete's turn. The Ottomans waged a titanic war to wrest the island from the Venetians. It began with raids on Haniá, Réthymno and Sitía in the 1530s by the notorious pirate-admiral Hayreddin Barbarossa.

Byzantine-style icon painting flourished under the Venetians

Over the next century, the Venetians greatly strengthened the fortifications, but Haniá and Réthymno fell anyway in 1645. Two years later, the Turks laid siege to the capital, Candia. It was an epic struggle, which was to last 22 years. Initially weakened by an outbreak of plague, the 12,000-strong population rallied to the defence. After fifteen years, the Turkish commander, Hüseyin Pasha, was summoned back to Constantinople and publicly strangled for his failure to take the city. Supposedly thirty thousand defenders died, but there were 118,000 fatalities among the besiegers.

Ottoman rule

Crete's years spent under the Ottomans (1669–1898) largely constituted a period of cultural and economic stagnation. Imperial leaders had no interest in developing or investing in this new domain and, after the occasionally oppressive but at times brilliant centuries of Venetian government, Crete slid back into a dark age.

Apart from repairing the islands' fortifications, the Ottomans left relatively few lasting remnants of their rule. They built few mosques – largely because many Cretan converts adhered to the heterodox Bektaşi sect – and left only a few houses in the largest towns, where they made up nearly half of the population until the

1840s. Most numerous of their legacies are the ornate street fountains found in the corners of market squares and outside chapels. Throughout this period, many town-dwelling Cretans kept a low profile. They publicly converted to Islam to escape taxes, continuing to practise their Orthodox faith in secret.

There were sporadic attempts at revolt, which were often launched from remote mountain strongholds where rebels could survive in safety. The more vulnerable communities on the lower plains paid a high price for these revolts in the form of swift and bloody reprisals.

The first major rebellion occurred in 1770 when the Russians, hoping to distract the Turks while they waged their own attacks on the Ottoman Empire elsewhere, promised aid to Daskalogiannis, a wealthy shipowner. He raised a revolt in Sfakiá, but the support never arrived. The rebellion was crushed, Daskalogiannis was flayed alive, and the event became the subject of a rousing epic poem.

However, once part of Greece had achieved independence from the Ottoman Empire after 1830, the atmosphere changed. After two decades of rule by an Egyptian vassal of the sultan, various forms of semi-autonomous rule, with representation for Christian notables, were attempted, but to no avail. Insurgencies recurred, generally put down with considerable severity; for the Cretan resisters, death came to form a monumental collective badge of honour.

During the major 1866 uprising, hundreds of Christian Cretans – and many Muslims – died in a suicide explosion at Arkádi

THE OUTCOME OF THE BATTLE FOR CRETE

Although Western Europe's leaders watched with bated breath, they sent little support, and inexorably Venetian resistance was worn down. As the conquerors entered the city gates in 1699, the Venetians negotiated an orderly departure, taking with them, among other Christian artefacts, the head of St Titus. This most cherished religious relic was not to return to the island until 1966.

The dead of two world wars lie in Haniá's British War Cemetery

Monastery. There were more insurgencies in 1889 and 1895. The island's repeated suffering was duly celebrated in the popular, heroic *Songs of Digenis* (adapted from their medieval origins for the modern struggle), Pandelis Prevelakis' particularly grim novel *The Cretan*, and the lofty writings of Níkos Kazantzákis.

Union with Greece

Finally, in 1898, the European powers forced the Ottomans to grant Crete autonomy within the empire and accept Prince George, second son of King George of Greece, as high commissioner. This did not satisfy Cretan nationalists, and the prince, presiding over an island divided into ultra-nationalist and accommodationist parliamentary factions, resigned in 1906. It was only in 1913, under the leadership of the Cretan Eleftherios Venizelos, that *énosis* (union) with Greece was achieved.

Despite being unscathed by World War I, Crete saw major changes between 1913 and the mid-1920s. Muslim Cretans had been leaving for Rhodes, the Middle East and Anatolia since 1897, but the disastrous 1919–22 Greek invasion of Turkey, and the ultimately successful Turkish resistance to it, greatly accelerated this movement through the compulsory population exchange between Greece and Turkey in 1923. The last of thousands of Muslims were expelled, with Orthodox refugees from Asia Minor arriving to take their place.

War and peace

Yet Crete's travails were not yet over. During World War II, the rapid advance of the German forces through mainland Greece in 1941 forced the Allies to retreat to Crete. On 20 May, German paratroopers secured the airfield at Máleme, just west of Haniá. British, Australian and New Zealand soldiers joined Cretan militia during a valiant defence in the ten-day Battle of Crete, but were ultimately forced to retreat across the island. Many were evacuated to Egypt, though several thousand were left stranded and fled to safety in the mountains. Casualties on both sides were terrible: Allied losses numbered two thousand killed and twelve thousand taken prisoner, while the German war cemetery contains almost 4,500 graves.

With a tradition of opposition to foreign invaders, Cretans immediately began resistance activities against the occupying German force. Initial efforts to shelter stranded Allied servicemen and smuggle them off the island in small groups from isolated south-coast beaches were remarkably successful. But after the Italian capitulation in September 1943, brutal German reprisals against civilians became more frequent. In early 1944, the resistance pulled off an amazing coup by kidnapping the German commander, General Kreipe, and smuggling him off the island. Subsequently, German forces burnt many villages and killed many men of fighting age in the Amári Valley. The occupation of Crete did not end until May 1945, when the Germans abandoned Haniá. Many towns were left in ruins from heavy bombing, but Crete largely escaped the internal strife of the civil war that raged in mainland Greece (1946–49) and felt fewer effects of the oppressive colonels' junta (1967–74) than other communities.

NOTES

Crete celebrates its National Day on 8 November, the anniversary of the explosion in 1866 at Arkádi Monastery, where hundreds of Cretan rebels died rather than surrender to the Turks.

In 1981, Greece became a full member of the European Community, and Andreas Papandreou's PASOK party, with overwhelming support from Crete (who saw it as heir to the Venizelist tradition), won elections to form Greece's first quasi-socialist government. Papandreou's son, George, became prime minister in 2009, presiding over economic collapse and charged with undoing most of his father's legacy, before being replaced by a technocratic unity coalition in 2011. In 2012, the leader of New Democracy Antonis Samaras became prime minister, and the country started pursuing further austerity measures. However, in 2014, the Greek unemployment rate rose to a record high of 28 percent.

In 2015, the Greeks turned from right-wing New Democracy to left-wing SYRIZA under Alexis Tsipras. Soon after holding a national referendum in the same year, Tsipras signed the Third bail-out agreement, according to which Greece would be given a loan of around 84 billion euros. In return, the country would have to introduce a number of reforms, including increasing VAT and privatizing a number of state assets. However, a group of MPs from SYRIZA heavily opposed these controversial reforms and stirred a party rebellion. After five months, Tsipras stepped down, only to return a month later.

The main church of Arkádi Monastery is a shrine to Cretan resistance

During his absence, Vassiliki Thanou-Christophilou stepped in to become the first female prime minister in Greece. In 2017, general and youth unemployment rates were 22 and 44 percent, respectively.

Faced with mounting disillusionment, SYRIZA's luck finally ran out when New Democracy were returned to power with almost 40 percent of the vote in the 2019 elections. Prime Minister Kyriakos Mistotakis, originally from Crete, followed with a raft of right-wing measures such as banning the right to strike.

Coronavirus effects

Kyriakos Mistotakis was praised for his government's initial handling of the 2020 global COVID-19 pandemic and his move to impose tough restrictions early on. The country was even able to open up for a short tourist season in 2020 and a longer one in 2021. Tourism bounced back robustly from 2022 onwards, with Crete enjoying a surge in arrivals. However, ongoing global inflation, partly triggered by the war in Ukraine, led to price hikes across the board and visitors may find today Crete rather pricier than before. On a positive note, this economic revival has funded upgrades to boutique hotels, expanded food offerings, and encouraged the growth of eco-conscious travel initiatives.

Ukraine War

Since the outbreak of the Ukraine War in the spring of 2022, Crete has experienced changes with both local and international dimensions, from military shifts to integrating an influx of Ukrainian refugees. The NATO base at Souda Bay gained heightened strategic importance with the US Navy and other allies. The most notable sign of this are the naval vessels docked here and military aircraft flying overhead, while community cultural events and festivals work to integrate Ukrainian nationals into daily life. While this has bolstered the local economy, some locals have concerns over rising militarisation. For travellers, it offers a rare glimpse into the island's role in geopolitics.

The Greek Prime Minister Kyriakos Mitsotakis

Climate

In October 2022, unusually heavy rainfall caused devastating flash floods in northern Crete, especially in seaside villages such as Agia Pelagia and Lygaria. Streets were inundated, vehicles were swept into the sea, and two lives were tragically lost. In the aftermath local authorities upgraded storm drainage systems and developed better emergency protocols. While tourism quickly resumed, travellers visiting in autumn are advised to monitor local forecasts.

Between 2023-24, in response to Europe's energy crisis Greece fast-tracked green energy projects, with Crete earmarked for expanded wind and solar installations. Wind farms were constructed in previously untouched areas of central and eastern Crete, sparking protests from environmental groups. Hikers in inland areas may now spot modern turbines juxtaposed against traditional landscapes.

A fast-moving wildfire ignited on 2 July 2025 near Ierapetra, along the southeastern coast of Crete – the island's largest – and quickly spread, fueled by gale-force winds (up to Beaufort 9). Over 1,500 people were evacuated into safer areas and some residents fled by sea and boat. Firefighting efforts were hampered by the persistent winds. Happily, no fatalities were recorded but there are valid fears that wildfires may become a regular threat.

Chronology

c.6500–2600BC Settlers arrive in Crete from Asia Minor.
2600–2000BC Pre-Palatial era: immigrants bring copper and pottery.
2000–1700BC Proto-Palatial period: discovery of bronze; language written down; first palaces built, then destroyed by earthquake.
1700–1450BC Neo-Palatial era: the height of Minoan civilisation.
c.1450BC Minoan palaces destroyed; Mycenaeans arrive.
c.1150BC Dorians from northern Greece conquer most of Crete.
67BC Crete becomes a Roman province, with Gortys the capital.
395 Roman Empire splits permanently, Crete allotted to Byzantium.
824–961 Arabs conquer Crete, destroy Gortys, make their capital at fortess of Rabdh el-Khandak (Iráklio).
961 Nikephoros Fokas recaptures Crete for Byzantium.
1204 Venetians acquire Crete, rule for 465 years from Candia (Iráklio).
1669 Turks capture Candia after 22-year siege and control all Crete.
1821–7 Greek War of Independence; Crete under Egyptian control.
1898 European Great Powers occupy Crete, which becomes an autonomous principality within the Ottoman Empire.
1913 Crete finally becomes part of Greece.
1923 Last Muslims expelled; Christians arrive from Asia Minor.
1941–5 Germany occupies Crete: heavy losses, villages destroyed.
1971 Iráklio replaces Haniá as capital of Crete.
1981 Greece joins the European Union. First socialist government.
2002 The euro becomes the currency of Greece.
2004 Greece hosts the Olympics in Athens.
2010–11 Greece effectively bankrupt, dependent on IMF/EU loans.
2014 Greek unemployment rises to a record high of 28 percent.
2015 The Greeks consent to the Third bailout agreement. Vassiliki Thanou-Christophilou becomes the first female PM.
2019 New Democracy return to power amidst continuing austerity.
2020–22 Covid-19 hits Greece.
2023–25 Tourism returns with rising prices. Crete plays a role in NATO related to the Ukraine War, while embracing refugees.

Haniá's Venetian harbour

Places

Crete is a big island – among the five largest in the Mediterranean – so if you want to see lots of what it has to offer, choose your itinerary carefully. Staying at a central base allows for excursions to both the east and west, whereas a base in the far east or west limits your ability to see the opposite end of the island easily.

This guide divides Crete into four sections: the capital, Iráklio, followed by the central section; then moving east, before finally exploring the western parts of the island. The major attractions are covered, so that you can plan your itinerary around them, but remember that the countryside is filled with hidden treasures; traditional communities, frescoed churches and mountain paths, all waiting to be discovered.

Iráklio

Highlights

- **The city centre**, see page 39
- **The harbour area**, see page 40
- **South of the city centre**, see page 41
- **The Archaeological Museum**, see page 42

Iráklio ❶ comes as a surprise to travellers used to Greek island ports further north in the Aegean Sea. It is the fourth-largest Greek city (population approximately 160,000), and the commercial and administrative heart of Crete. Despite current hard times – winter unemployment exceeds 25 percent – there is a lively scene based around its university, and a sophistication to match other medium-sized mainland Greek university towns, such as Pátra or Ioánnina. However, this is not the only facet of the city. Around the harbour you'll still find a fishing industry based on small family-owned boats, and in the narrow backstreets a few surviving small workshops.

Truth be told, Iráklio isn't a particularly attractive town; heavy bombing during World War II was compounded by thoughtless postwar development, and only recently have its crumbling medieval quarters, public monuments and surviving older buildings received the preservation attention they deserve. Spend little time here, and be sure to take what time you do spend exploring the narrow lanes beyond the traffic-clogged main boulevards, you'll be rewarded.

Nevertheless, it was a thriving port in Minoan times and became known as Heracleum under Roman rule. The Andalusians, who established the Emirate of Crete, built a huge castle here while the Venetians chose it as their capital, giving the name Candia to both the city and the whole island. Candia prospered from Venetian trade and when Turkish forces stormed the island, the town held out for 22 years before falling in 1669. As Kandiye, it became a relative backwater of the Ottoman Empire, only to rise to prominence again following union with Greece. It was declared capital again in 1971, taking the title from Haniá in the west. It is also worth mentioning that Iráklio is the birthplace of the painter El Greco, whose real name was Doménikos Theotokópoulos.

The Venetian fortress guards the harbour at Iráklio

The city centre

The city centre lies within the vast fortress started by the Venetians and reinforced by the Ottomans. One can walk along sections of its walls to gain an impression of how large the citadel once was. The heart of Iráklio is the small **Platía Venizélou** (Venizelos Square), with its fringe of cafés and restaurants. At its centre, the **Morosini Fountain** Ⓐ dates from Venetian times, though its sombre lion statues are three hundred years older and lend the widely used nickname of Platía Leondária (Lions' Square). From here, most of Iráklio's attractions are only a few minutes' walk – the closest, which flanks the plaza, being **Ágios Márkos** Ⓑ (St Mark's), a Venetian church built in 1239, now the municipal art gallery (heraklionartgallery.gr/art-gallery; free) showcasing paintings, sculptures, and engravings that highlight the evolution of Cretan and Greek art – from the lyrical Renaissance to the twentieth century.

NOTES

Iráklio was first named Heracleum by the Romans, before the Andalucian Arabs changed its name to Rabdh-al-Khandaq – becoming Hándax for the Greeks under Nikephoros Phokas who soon re-conquered it. The Venetians renamed it Candia. During the Ottoman occupation, Muslims knew it as Kandiye, while the Cretans called it Megalo Kastro (Big Fortress), until the name Iráklio was officially adopted in 1913.

North along the pedestrianised Ikostipémptis Avgoústou (25th August Street) looms the impressive façade of the **Venetian Loggia**, originally dating from 1628 but reconstructed after World War II. Iráklio's municipal offices divide themselves between here and the adjacent Andrógeio Mégaro. Walk around the loggia to find the **Church of Ágios Títos** Ⓒ. Founded late in the first millennium, it honours St Titus, the island's first bishop and patron saint. When the church was consecrated, Titus's body was brought here from Gortys and re-interred. The Venetians took his remains

The market on 1866 Street

to Venice when they fled the island and the church was rebuilt as the Vezir Mosque after an 1856 earthquake, resulting in the incongruous but beautiful decoration on the outer walls. In 1966 the Venetian authorities returned the skull of St Titus to Ágios Títos in a gold reliquary, along with fine paintings depicting scenes of the saint's life. Just west lies a small park supplied with more cafés.

The harbour area

Continuing down 25th August Street leads to the waterfront and the majestic **Koulés** Venetian fortress Ⓓ (http://koules.efah.gr; charge) out on the breakwater, built to protect the old harbour. En route you'll pass vaulted remains of the large, arcaded **arsenália** (repair depots) that serviced Venetian ships, and the city's fishing fleet – small colourful boats with piles of yellow nets. The fortress was completed in 1540 to protect the town against the Ottoman threat and, with the circuit of walls inland, explains how Candia held out long after the rest of Crete had fallen. The fortress was reopened in 2016 with a completely new exhibition presenting the history of the edifice. A tour of the interior reveals a strong and efficient design; there are wonderful views from its ramparts.

A short walk west along the waterfront, past the disused Dominican monastery of Ágios Pétros (St Peter), brings you to the **Historical Museum of Crete** Ⓔ (https://historical-museum.

gr; charge), housed in an impressive building that is part Venetian mansion, part modern glass edifice. The museum – thematically rather than chronologically – covers Cretan history from the Byzantine Empire to the present, as well as ethnography. There are exquisite icons and fresco fragments rescued from churches across the island, stone relief carvings, documentation of the local Jewish, Muslim and Armenian communities, folk textiles and a re-creation of a traditional Cretan home. Models and prints of Iráklio across the centuries show how the townscape has developed, as does an interactive model of the medieval city, showing the many monuments sadly destroyed since 1897. Due prominence is given to the struggle for Cretan independence and World War II resistance (including the 1942 sabotage of the local German airfield), as well as the only two, small El Greco paintings still on Crete.

The **Natural History Museum of Crete** **F** (https://nhmc.uoc.gr; charge) lies just west, housed in a former seafront power plant. The museum has interesting displays of flora and fauna as well as an earthquake simulator, where visitors can experience an earthquake of magnitude up to six degrees on the Richter scale (there are sessions every half hour).

South of the city centre

South of Lions' Square is **1866 Street**, nicknamed 'Market Street', which still retains some of the atmosphere of an old bazaar. Here you can stroll past stalls selling fresh produce and souvenirs or eat at the numerous *ouzeris* that serve the market workers. At the southern end of Market Street is **Platía Kornárou** **G** (Kornárou Square) where you will find a hexagonal Ottoman pumphouse (now a café) beside the **Bembo Fountain** (Kríni Bémbou), created in 1588 using numerous pieces of architectural spolia, including the torso of a Roman statue.

A short walk northwest from here along the inner arterial road brings you to **Platía Agías Ekaterínis** (St Catherine's Square) where the nineteenth-century cathedral of Ágios Minás dwarfs two older religious buildings. The small church immediately adjacent is also called **Ágios Minás**, with a splendidly ornate iconostasis – if the church is closed, ask in the cathedral for the key. Behind these two churches is the 15th-century shrine that gives the square its name: **Agía Ekateríni** (St Catherine). It originally belonged to St Catherine's monastery in the Egyptian Sinai, and served as a monastic school. Today it houses the **St Catherine's Museum** **H**, also known as the **Museum of Christian Art** (http://iakm.gr/agia; charge), with a wealth of art from churches and monasteries across the island, including six large icons by the celebrated Cretan artist Mihaïl Damaskinos.

The Archaeological Museum

Walk southeast from Lions' Square along the pedestrianised shopping street, Dedálou, to reach the city's top attraction, the **Archaeological Museum of Iráklio** **I** (https://heraklionmuseum.gr/en; charge). One of the greatest archeological collections in the world, this brings together finds from sites across Crete and from every era of the island's ancient history. Pride of place goes to the best Minoan artefacts.

As the pre-eminent centre of this ancient people, Crete is the main source of information and excavated remains concerning the Minoans. For any other museum this would be treasure enough, yet there are also impressive Greek and Roman artefacts to enjoy. The extensively renovated museum is a must for those intending to visit the ancient sites, since the objects here add life to the now-empty cities and palaces. To fully appreciate its glories will take several hours – the exquisite detail on pottery and frescoes, and the fine workmanship in jewellery and everyday tools is breathtaking. Try to visit in the early morning or late afternoon to avoid the large tour groups who arrive at around midday. The 24 rooms are arranged in chronological order from the Neolithic to the Roman period, grouping artefacts from each site; only a room devoted to Minoan wall-paintings and sculptures breaks this chronological arrangement. Below are some of the highlights of your tour.

Hagios Markos is a former Roman catholic church in the center of Heraklion city

The earliest finds are from 7000BC (Neolithic and Pre-Palatial periods). Many were found at Móhlos on the northeastern coast. Primitive pottery is on display – including a rather naive clay bull with an acrobat holding one horn – and finer work such as a stone *pyxis* (jewellery box) incised with geometric patterns and a reclining animal.

Finds from the Proto-Palatial period (2000–1700BC) include the earliest examples of fine Kamáres ware pottery, found in the ruins at Knossos. Fascinating miniature work is also in evidence, with a series of tiny faience plaques depicting the façades of Minoan houses.

The finest find uncovered at the Phaistos Palace is **Phaistos Disc**, a clay disc 16cm (6.25in) in diameter, imprinted with hieroglyphic and geometric symbols that have yet to be deciphered.

Finds from the golden age of Minoan society – the Neo-Palatial period (1700–1450BC) – include artefacts originated in the palaces of Knossos, Mália and Phaistos. It is worth mentioning the superb *rhyton* (libation vessel) carved from black steatite in the shape of a

WHERE TO TAKE THE BEST PICTURES

Crete offers a stunning mix of natural beauty and archaeological wonders, perfect for photo enthusiasts. At **Elafonísi Beach**, head to the sandbar at sunset for dreamlike reflections and glowing pink sands; the shallow water allows for shots looking back toward shore. Use a waterproof camera and bring a picnic. **Váï Beach** dazzles with its palm-fringed shores and oasis-like feel. Snap sunrise photos from the hill trails at either end of the beach – avoid heavy gear due to the climb. Inland, the **Lasíthi Plateau** rewards early risers with sunrise vistas over fertile plains and dramatic mountain peaks–zoom lenses are ideal. At **Phaistos**, shoot panoramic photos from the hilltop above this unspoiled Minoan site, capturing Mt Psiloritis and the palace ruins. For dramatic landscapes, hike **Samaria Gorge** at first light. The Iron Gates – narrow yet towering cliffs – are unforgettable photo spots. Travel light due to the 16km hike. Finally, visit **Gourniá** early for serene shots of ancient Minoan ruins. The best overview is from the road above the site. Combine with nearby **Voulisma Beach** for a full, photogenic day.

bull's head. The bull was one of the foremost religious symbols of the Minoans and this piece was created by one of the pre-eminent artisans of the time.

There are also objects from the final phase of Minoan civilisation (1450–1400BC) on display. The pottery and stonework are worth a look, but the principal artefacts of interest are the Linear A script fragments incised on thin clay plates and not yet deciphered and the examples of Linear B script, which were deciphered in 1952 and are of Mycenaean origin. The Linear B findings show that by the time the tablet was written the Minoans had already lost control of the major cities.

Also on display here is a delightful clay model of a Minoan dwelling, complete with roof terrace and tiny windows to keep out the bright sun and fierce Cretan winds.

Tomb finds that date from the Neo-Palatial and Post-Palatial periods include beautiful pottery pieces, military artefacts such as helmets and sword handles, and splendid gold jewellery.

The collection of domestic utensils and personal objects found in the palaces and around the *Megara* (royal chambers) includes stone vessels, pottery, hammers and a potter's wheel. There are several intricately carved steatite vessels, including the **Harvester Vase** discovered at Agía Triáda and decorated with a low relief of men at work in the fields.

A number of items come from the palace of Zakros in the far east of Crete. The 'marine' amphora is decorated with octopuses and Argonauts. A delicate rock-crystal *rhyton* shows the sophistication of both workmanship and personal taste in the Neo-Palatial period. There are finds from other sites in eastern Crete, artefacts from the Post-Palatial period (1400–1100BC), and the period between 1100BC and 650BC, including a large collection of gold jewellery. A string of painted Minoan sarcophagi, many decorated with the images of fish or birds, are displayed.

The Archaeological Museum of Iráklio is the place to see the finest surviving **frescoes** found throughout the Minoan kingdoms, dating from 1600 to 1400. They depict the

The windmills of Lasithi Plateau

enigmatic Minoans at work and play, and their major influences – the bull, other animals and the marine environment. Male figures – presumably out in the sun more – were always rust coloured, while more secluded females were always painted white.

The spiral decoration of the only stone **sarcophagus** found on the island (at Agía Triáda) frames scenes of libation and other religious activities. You can also examine a miniature re-creation of the palace of Knossos, completed according to early hypotheses on its design.

The **Ring of King Minos** is an engraved Minoan gold ring found in 1928 close to the Knossos palace, and long considered to be a hoax before being verified by experts in 2002.

The Agía Triáda sarcophagus shows tributes imported from Africa

The museum has a shop (as of Nov'24 closed for renovations), which sells books and postcards, a café and there are several more just across the street from the entrance. You'll find the main busy main tourist office in Lions Square in the standout yellow arched building, known as the Aktarika Building (https://heraklion.gr/en/visitor).

A treat for contemporary art-lovers is the Museum of Visual and Fine Arts (https://metheraklion.gr; free), located at Nymphon 3, further east from the Archaeological Museum.

Housed in a former basilica, it exhibits works from the finest contemporary artists of Cretan descent.

Central Crete

Highlights

Central Crete is the market garden and vineyard of the island, with fertile valleys nestling between rocky mountain ranges. Today it supplies much of the fresh produce for the population, including grapes for the quaffable Cretan country wine. This is not a recent development: it was home to the Minoans, with their most famous palace only a few kilometres away from Iráklio. The Roman capital was also located in this region. Around these important archeological sites are farming communities quite different in character from the city and the coastal resorts. Spend time exploring these villages for a glimpse of a lifestyle that will soon disappear as the younger generation forsakes rural ways of life.

Knossos

Just 5km (3 miles) south of Iráklio is **Knossos** ❷ (https://knossos-palace.gr; charge – book tickets in advance online), now famed worldwide as the place where Sir Arthur Evans (at that time Director of the Ashmolean Museum in Oxford) found proof that the mythical ancient civilisation of Crete had really existed. Evans named this people the Minoans after their most-famous, semi-mythical king – Minos. He began digging in 1900 after buying the

MINOAN BUILDING METHODS

Knossos construction methods were complicated, with light wells illuminating lower chambers, and polythyra, masonry supports to create structural integrity, between which were large wooden doors serving as partitions. Cypress or juniper trunks served as anti-seismic cushioning in walls, and the same wood (often poised upside down) used as columns. Many quarters were semi-subterranean for more comfort in the warm climate, with high windows for ventilation.

site, financing the excavation programme with his own money, and almost immediately struck the first masonry of a huge Bronze Age palace replete with magnificent pottery and other artefacts.

Evans' subsequent attempts to reconstruct areas of the palace have met with intense criticism from other scholars but Knossos (Knossós in modern Greek) is now Crete's premier attraction, and rightly so. Although there is no documented proof, the majority of Cretans believe that Knossos was the site of the famed battle between Theseus and the Minotaur in the Labryinth below King Minos's palace.

The first palace at Knossos was built *c.*2000BC in the Proto-Palatial era, but this was destroyed by a massive earthquake only three hundred years later. Most of what you see here today are the remains of the second palace, built following the disaster. This coincided with a golden age of Minoan society (the Neo-Palatial era, from 1700BC), when the people grew rich through trade and artistic endeavour was at its peak. The palace expanded continuously through the following years, resulting in a complex of around 1,200 small rooms several storeys high covering over 20,000 sq m (215,280 sq ft). This golden era came to an end in 1450BC, and major fire caused catastrophic damage around 1350BC, but although the palace was completely destroyed, the surrounding town continued to be occupied until the fifth century AD.

The palace was erected around a large **Central Court**, possibly used for public meetings, which now forms the heart of the site. Imagine Minoans at play here as depicted on the pottery and frescoes in the Archaeological Museum in Iráklio – acrobats and dancers as well as the famed bull-leapers. Visitors enter past what remains of the **West Court**, used as an entryway to a **West Wing**, where the administrative and religious activities took place. Minoans would walk down the corridor of processions past frescoed walls to reach the **propylaea** (sacred entranceway). A **grand staircase** then led north to the most important official chambers within this wing, its sturdy painted colonnades typical of those found throughout the palace.

The lower floor here houses the **throne room**, with ornate griffin frescoes and a lustral basin for ritual purification. The walls – lined with stone seats thought to have been used by advisers or councillors – would have been decorated with red plaster and an ornamental dado. In the northeastern corner was a crypt where a cache of treasures was unearthed during the excavations.

A staircase by the throne room leads to what Evans christened the **piano nobile** – a reconstructed upper floor of the west wing. Next to the staircase is the

A lustral basin at Knossos Palace

Huge jars called píthi were used to store grain, oil, wine or water

Tripartite Shrine where the Linear B alphabetical tablets were discovered.

On the east side of the court, a **grand staircase** leads to the royal chambers or *Megara*, where some of the best-preserved rooms can be found. The shallow gypsum staircase is a stunning construction and one of the masterpieces of Minoan architecture. Notice the clever use of lighting wells to illuminate the lowest storeys (there were four in total). The **King's Megaron** is decorated with a simple wooden throne, although the antechamber walls are incised with images of the double axe or *labrys*, so important to the mythology surrounding Knossos. The room is also known as the **Hall of the Double Axes**. The architecture of this room is typically Neo-Palatial in style, with large *polythyra* supporting the roof. It is thought that large wooden doors were fitted between the pillars and that these could be removed to create a *stoa* (open-fronted arcade), if the king wished it. The **Queen's Megaron** has a splendid dolphin fresco lining one wall. On the far side of the site are the remains of the Royal Road leading north to the coast, still in exceptional condition.

Evans made numerous remarkable finds at the site, since it had been covered and left undisturbed following the 1350BC disaster. Pottery intricately painted with marine life, bronze figurines and exquisite jewels – many of these were discovered in the rock-cut tombs of the Post-Palatial period. Yet it is the mundane and simple things that make Knossos so fascinating. Evidence of early water piping, central heating and sanitation show a remarkable sophistication.

Towards Gortys (Górtyna)

Other classical sites lay below Iráklio near the south coast. The **Nikos Kazantzakis Museum** (Myrtia; https://kazantzaki.gr/en; charge) is located around 6km (4 miles) south of Knossos. The museum exhibits the intellectual heritage of one of the most acknowledged Cretan author and philosopher, Nikos Kazantzakis.

Take the road southwest to **Agía Varvára**, in a vine-filled valley skirting the looming Psiloritis range to the west. Beyond lies the **Mesará Plain**, a wide fertile valley surrounded by hills and a centre for farming since ancient times. For a pretty drive through the foothills on the north, take the direct road to **Zarós** ❸ from Agía Varvára. The scenery is magnificent, with plenty to do locally: idle by the **Votamós lake**, hike the **Rouvás Gorge** just north, or visit the small, frescoed **Moní Vrondisíou** (https://unescositesincrete.

RITES AND SACRIFICES

In the Minoan civilisation, the bull symbolised virility and all natural forces. The walls of the palace of Knossos are covered in paintings and sculptures of huge sacred horns. In the courtyard, young people used to perform an acrobatic game where they had to grab the bull's horns and leap above the animal. Every year, a bull was caught, its throat slit and its blood collected. This sacrifice bound Minoan society and the animal's divine powers to the great cycles of nature. The Mother Goddess was represented by the Snake Goddess's bare breasts, a symbol of fertility. The snake itself was a symbol of reincarnation and healing. The sacred pillar embodied the goddess, while the double-headed axe represented the moon and the double power – religious and political – of the priest-king.

gr/en/simeia-endiaferontos/vrontisi-monastery; free), 4km (2.5 miles) away on the **Kamáres** road, the original home of the Damaskinos icons, now in Agía Ekateríni in Iráklio. Visitors, as in any monastery, are expected to dress modestly and cover shoulders and knees.

Further, at Vorízia, you'll find the turning for **Ágios Fanoúrios** (Varsamónero; free), another monastic church with vivid fifteenth-century frescoes. Beyond Kamáres, with its famous cave overhead, the same road continues towards the Amári Valley to the west (see page 80).

To reach the ancient sites drop directly down from Agía Varvára to the Mesará. Near **Ágii Déka** – named after ten saints who were martyred here, and whose purported catacomb is still viewable at the village's west edge – are the ancient remains of **Gortys** ❹ (Górtyna), capital of the island during the Roman era (from 67BC) but already an important city in Minoan times.

Gortys is such a huge site – at its height it had a population of 300,000 – that you will see signposts to remains lying amidst olive groves, south of the modern road. By following the signage, you will be rewarded with ancient columns resting against olive trees,

KAMÁRES POTTERY

Kamáres vases date from the Proto-Palatial Period, deriving their name from the Kamáres cave on the southern flank of the Psiloritis range, where they were first found. The characteristic features are polychrome paintings on a dark background. Motifs from nature such as spirals and rosettes combine to create a harmonious unity.

Neo-Palatial Period vases of the so-called floral style display leaves or other plant motifs, while marine-style vessels are covered with octopuses, paper nautilus or even coral designs. These vessels were either buried with the dead, given as votive offerings or else used as crockery in the palaces where they were found.

shards of pottery among the grass, and a governor's palace and amphitheatre to explore.

The fenced main site (charge) covers only a tiny part of the city, but it protects one of the most important archeological finds on Crete – the **Law Code** dating from the Dorian period, around 500BC. This huge stone tablet was incised with script setting forth the rules on marriage, criminal justice, property and inheritance rights. The tablet is incorporated into the rear of a small Roman **odeion**. The site entrance is dominated by the triple apse of the sixth-century **Basilica of Ágios Títos** (St Titus), all that remains after Arab raiders razed most of the building in AD 825.

Ruins of sixth-century Basilica of Ágios Títos at Gortys

Phaistos

Travel on through the village of Mires to reach **Phaistos** ❺ (Festós), the site of an impressive Minoan palace (https://minoancrete.com/phaistos.html; charge). As Gortys rose in prominence towards the end of the first millennium BC, the fortunes of Phaistos declined, though it had been the seat of power for most of southern Crete in Minoan times.

Phaistos is probably the most dramatic Minoan site on the entire island. Its palace is set on top of a rocky knoll with rooms cascading down the hillside. There are sweeping views out across the plain to Mt Psiloritis on the north and the Asteroúsia range to the south. In legend, King Minos installed his brother Rhadamanthys as ruler here. He was known as a wise and honest man consulted by many as an arbitrator.

The layout of the palace is similar to that of Knossos, but here there has been no reconstruction. Instead, the remains of three successive palaces – two from the Proto-Palatial era and one from the Neo-Palatial era – can be seen, with almost nothing standing more than a metre above the ground. You enter the site down a flight of steps and find yourself in the **west court**, which doubled as a **theatral area**. The remains downhill to the south are of one of the old palaces, just below are the walls of the new palace. You'll see scant remains of a shrine, with kiln-like storage pits whose function is uncertain. On the east side of the west court, the **grand stairway** leads to the **propylon**, the entryway into the newer palace. The **west wing** – as at Knossos – was chiefly made up of shrines and storerooms, and many objects of ritual use were found during excavations here. Some rooms still house their lustral bowls for ritual purification.

Phaistos Minoan site

Beyond all this extends the vast **central courtyard** at the southeast corner of the site. From here, you head north towards the royal chambers – two giant *píthi* (large earthenware pots) guard the entryway from the central court. You'll find a peristyle hall here (off limits) and steps leading down to the **King's and Queen's chambers** – both built to make the most of the cooling updrafts of the hillside. The east court was mainly used for practical activities, as there are remnants of a furnace and workshops here – perhaps for copper smelting. They would have supplied the palace with its need for ceremonial or funerary articles.

The **Phaistos disc** was discovered here by workers in 1903 in a tiny, apparently insignificant, clay-walled chamber on the northern edge of the site. The disc, apparently dating from around 1700BC, is covered with a spiral pattern of symbols and geometric forms that have yet to be deciphered. The original lies in Iráklio's Archaeological Museum (see page 42) – though plenty of replicas are on sale at the Phaistos site shop.

Agía Triáda and Vóri

Just 3km (2 miles) beyond Phaistos on the same road is **Agía Triáda** (charge), built – archeologists believe – as a summer palace for the royal court and linked with Phaistos by Minoan road. Set on a hillside overlooking the Gulf of Mesará it offered excellent views and cooling breezes, as the sea came much closer in those days. The remains indicate modules of rooms that could work either as a whole or individually – perhaps to accommodate varying sizes of entourage at different times. The west wing housed the royal quarters.

Agía Triáda (original name unknown) was built late in the Minoan era, *c.*1700BC and although it suffered great damage in the cataclysm of 1450BC, it was reoccupied, and a Dorian town was built to one side, its agora still evident. Since the Minoan settlement was famed for several shrines, scholars have debated that the original palace may have had some religious purpose.

Archaeological site of Agía Triáda

Numerous tombs have been excavated on the hillside, and the sarcophagus in the Iráklio museum, finely decorated with cult scenes, was found here. Atop the whole site is the incongruous fourteenth-century church of **Ágios Geórgios** (always open), with fresco fragments inside.

Just 3km from Phaistos, north of the main road, the traditional village of **Vóri** ❻ has clusters of old houses, a central square and an excellent, if spottily labelled, two-storey **Museum of Cretan Ethnology** (https://cretanethnologymuseum.gr; charge) near the main church. It's an antique-dealers dream of old furniture, weavings and tools touching on every aspect of rural life, from pig-butchery to bootmaking. Look out for eel traps and animal muzzles made of basketry, an all-wood wheelbarrow and the giant smithy bellows.

Mátala to Agía Galíni

A more frequented lunch-and-swim stop is the coastal resort of **Mátala** ❼, about 11km (7 miles) southwest of Phaistos. Here you'll find a good sandy bay lined with tavernas. The waters are well regarded by snorkellers and there are fascinating remains of a barely submerged Roman port. On the northern side are high sandstone cliffs where you will find many large **Roman tombs**, better known as the **Ancient City of Mátala** (https://allincrete.

com/matala-caves; charge) cut into the rock. Until the late 1970s, these man-made caves were unprotected and used as free camping spots by legions of countercultural travellers. Today they are fenced-off and cleared out at dusk.

For a calmer, less commercial alternative, try **Léndas** ❽ and its long west beach, 23km (14 miles) south from Ágii Déka village beyond the outriders of Asteroúsia. It's too far to fit into most day-outings, so you'll want to spend the night.

Travelling west from the Mesará you'll reach the coastal resort of **Agía Galíni** ❾, its buildings tumbling down a hill to a tiny port from which you can take boat excursions along the coast, the best of these to spectacular **Ágios Pávlos** beach, with a huge dune backing it. North from Agía Galíni the main road leads to Réthymno (see page 75).

The central mountains

Heading west out of Iráklio you can take the relatively fast New National Road along the coast, with easy links to the resorts of **Agía Pelagía, Balí** and (best) **Pánormos**, or the slower Old National Road, which winds its way inland via Damásta and Pérama. The slow route allows you to explore some of the most rugged and interesting landscapes in Crete, and leads you back to mythological times when the gods ruled the earth. The **Psiloritis range** ❿ dominates central Crete, rising steeply to the chapel of Timiós Stavrós (Holy Cross) on the highest peak – Óros Ídi (Mt Ida) is a distinguished 2,456m (8,056ft) in elevation. In summer the long summit ridge seems almost to touch the clear azure sky; in winter it attracts a mantle

NOTES

There are more than three thousand caves in Crete – approximately half of all the caves in Greece. This is due to the porous, water-soluble properties of the island's limestone strata.

of snow and thick menacing clouds, and the foothill villages seem to hang suspended on this swirling grey blanket. Climbing the peak takes around eight hours (round trip) from the Nída Plateau at the base of the ridge, in turn reached on foot from Zarós or Kamáres, or by path or road from Anógia. Between May and June is the best season, when days are long and snow is minimal. Essential equipment includes Loraine Wilson's *The High Mountains of Crete*, which thoroughly documents all alternatives.

The men and women of this region have been among the most stalwart against Crete's enemies, and subject to some of their worst reprisals – none more so than the inhabitants of the village of **Anógia** ⓫. The population suffered two bloody occasions under the Ottomans when the village was razed to the ground, and again in World War II. After Cretan and British partisans kidnapped General Kreipe, head of the occupying forces on the island, German soldiers marched into the village, killing all the men and burning houses. Several monuments in the village commemorate these sad events. Through happier times the village has built a reputation for weaving and embroidery – still sold in the lower town – as well as for its musicians (especially the Xylouris clan). This is one place where you will

View of Anógia village

probably see men in their traditional costume of *stivánia* (high leather boots), *vrákes* (baggy breeches) and *saríki* (headband).

Anógia, on a separate secondary route above the old national road, is a popular point of entry to Psiloritis. Follow a paved road out of the top of the village towards the Nída Plateau, once visited only by shepherds tending their flocks. From there, it's only a short walk to the **Idaean Cave** (Idéon Andron) where in legend the god Zeus spent his childhood, protected from his father Kronos by fierce, shield-banging warriors, the *kouretes*. Though the cave itself is not very impressive, it held a powerful sway over its ancient people; archeologists have found votive offerings dating back over three thousand years.

Eastern Crete

Highlights

This part of Crete offers contrasting landscapes. Some of the longest-established resorts sprawl along the northern coast, while inland, verdant valleys divide mountain ranges that were trackless until the 1970s. Here, it is still just possible to find the traditional rural lifestyle once omnipresent in the interior of the island. Caves, gorges and ancient sites add to the attraction, and make the east a good location for a combination beach/excursion holiday.

Rowdy resorts

Heading out from Iráklio, you'll pass the airport some 5km (3 miles) away before reaching the beginning of the coastal strip. The New National Road takes you swiftly along, so if you want to explore, take the Old National Road where it still exists. This part of the northern coast was the main target of development during the 1970s and 1980s, and it is not to everyone's taste. Large concrete hotels and apartments make up a home from home for many European nationals, with English, German and Dutch menus, satellite football and all the favourite northern European TV programmes. At times it's hard to believe that you are on a Greek island. However, if you want almost nonstop fun, then this is the place for you. Waterparks, bungee-jumping, go-karting, bars and nightclubs – it's all here.

Mália to Neápoli

En route to Mália you may want to visit the **Lychnostatis open-air museum** (Hersonisso; https://lychnostatis.gr; charge), which is dedicated to Cretan flora, folk art and ethnography. The development reaches a peak at **Liménas Hersonísou** ⓬, although the inland village of **Ano Hersónisos** still has vestiges of its old atmosphere – and some Cretan tavernas. Liménas rivals **Mália** ⓭ as the island's clubbing capital, famous for fine beaches and also home to the tranquil Minoan **Palace of Mália** (https://minoancrete.com/malia.htm; charge), in farmland close to the sea around 2km (1 mile) east of town.

Remains under and around the palace indicate Neolithic settlements, although the first palace was built after 2000BC (later than Knossos and Phaistos) and it revealed no Kamáresware pottery from the Pre-Palatial period like that found at the other palaces. Its design is also simpler, with no large halls or fine wall decorations. This first palace was destroyed by an earthquake *c.*1700BC; there are scant remains of it on the northwest of the site.

The new palace centred on an open courtyard with a **west wing** mainly consisting of storerooms and cult rooms. A loggia fronted the square on this wing. In one room a *píthos* was found with a ceremonial dagger inside, and alongside this lay a sword decorated with gold and crystal, leading scholars to conclude that this was a preparation or contemplation room for the king. Up a nearby flight of stairs is an **altar room** with the base of its altar table still in situ.

Further west a *polythron* area with a paved floor is thought to have been the **royal apartments**. Hieroglyphic clay tablets and official seals were found here. Just a little way north of the palace site is the **chrysólakkos** or 'pit of gold', a mausoleum where the much-prized golden bee pendant was discovered among a larger cache of jewels. Archeologists are now busy excavating the extensive town that surrounded the palace and parts of this – on the palace's northwest flank – can be viewed from an overhead walkway.

Soon after ancient Mália the road turns inland past the town of **Neápoli**, birthplace of Petros Philargos, who, raised as a Catholic, became Pope Alexander V in 1409 – or rather, the Pisan 'antipope', as there were three rival claimants to the papacy at the time. This is the only place on the island where you can try *soumáda*,

Píthi amongst the ruins of Mália's Minoan palace

The shore of Lake Voulisméni, Ágios Nikólaos

a sweet drink made from wild almonds. It was capital of Lasíthi district before Ágios Nikólaos, and still marks the start of a scenic road up to the eponymous plateau.

Ágios Nikólaos

Eventually new and old highways meet the coast again at **Ágios Nikólaos** ⓮, probably the pleasantest town in eastern Crete. Though Agios Nikólaos – known to many Brits as 'Ag Nik' – suffered from a rash of ugly buildings going up in the 1970s, it has since made an effort to retain its character, and offers a more Greek atmosphere than the Mália/Liménas Hersonísou strip.

The town sits on the **Gulf of Mirabéllo**, blanketing low hills that rise up from the shoreline. At the centre of town is **Lake Voulisméni**, a 60-metre-deep spring-fed lake where a plethora of pretty fishing boats are tied. Numerous cafés and tavernas line the north and eastern edges of the lake, and you can sit and watch kingfishers swoop for minnows or divers descend to the bluey-green depths.

The south and west sides of the lake are flanked by sheer rock faces and you can climb the steps to the top for superb views over the town – perfect at sunset.

Lake Voulisméni is connected to the sea by an artificial channel. Across the road bridge at its mouth is the main tourist office, and beyond is the main port – where ferries no longer call. From the quay just beyond the bridge, excursion boats ply to local attractions, though it's a very long way to Spinalónga (see page 64).

You won't be able to explore Ágios Nikólaos without climbing a few hills. Shops selling upmarket clothing line the harbourside and Mt Skafianá, leading to Kitroplatía cove. Part-pedestrianised Ikosiogdóis Oktovríou makes for another pleasant stroll towards the central plaza.

The local **Archaeological Museum**, (https://agiosnikolaoscrete.com/experiences/culture/museums-sights/archaeological-museum-of-agios-nikolaos; charge) near the top of Konstandínou Paleológou keeps a good collection of Minoan artefacts, presented in chronological order such as a sarcophagus with skeleton still in place, and the 'Goddess of Myrtos', an exquisite libation vessel dating from the 2nd millennium BC in the shape of a woman with a long neck and squat body. A later Roman find is the skull from Potamós, decorated with a crown of gold olive leaves. The coin nearby was found between the skull's teeth, presumably the dead man's fare to the ferryman across the River Styx to the underworld.

Eloúnda to Spinalónga island

Ágios Nikólaos doesn't have great beaches; Havánia just west of town, and Almyrós 2km (1 mile) south, are serviceable at best. As a result, much of its upmarket accommodation lies north along the coast towards **Káto Eloúnda**. This coastal resort is understated, with a pretty church on the waterfront. You can also head to Spinalónga island from here – a much shorter trip than from Ágios Nikólaos. Don't confuse it with Cape Spinalónga which is accessible from Eloúnda via a narrow causeway over an artificial canal.

In the shallows around the causeway are the remains of the Greco-Roman city of **Oloús**, still flourishing during the second century AD, according to Greek geographer Pausanias. It probably sank during tectonic upheavals in the fourth century, which did spare an early Christian basilica (fenced off) inland, whose floor mosaics include frolicking dolphins.

Further north on the mainland, the tiny coastal resort of **Pláka** has the quickest, cheapest boat transfer (9am–6pm every half hour in season; https://spinalonga-island.gr; charge) to Spinalónga island, directly offshore. Weekends are very busy – best to embark before 11am – and take a hat and liquids as there's no shade or refreshment on the island. **Spinalónga island** ⓯ (free entry but must pay boat to reach) is girded with the bastions and curtain walls of the Venetian stronghold, built in 1579 to protect the entrance to the sheltered bay behind; a late Ottoman town on the sheltered, landward side; and the leper colony that later occupied it. The fortress was never taken by force; the Venetian garrison remained here until 1715, over sixty years after the fall of Iráklio, and left only after a treaty gave them safe passage. Muslim Cretans in turn retreated to the island when they came under threat from Cretan rebels at the end of the nineteenth century.

In 1903, the Cretan administrative council decided to establish a leper colony here; whether this was to force the Muslim villagers to leave is debatable, but the disease was rampant on the main island, and Spinalónga's position – offshore yet not too remote – was considered ideal for quarantining its sufferers. Initially, the

OVERNIGHT SENSATION

The 2010 Greek television series *To Nisi* (*The Island*), based on Victoria Hislop's novel of the same name, has been a huge success, resulting in a continuing traffic of visitors to the Spinalónga area. It was shot mostly at Pláka and the hillside village of Páno Eloúnda, as the archeological authorities did not let Mega Channel's crew use the island itself as a location. The sets at Pláka are now dismantled, but at Páno Eloúnda they have been left as a tourist attraction, cleverly intermingled with the original houses. Wandering the attractive streets, you can see why the village, with its sweeping views, was chosen.

regime was harsh, with victims treated more like criminals than patients; however, conditions improved over the years, thanks to patient activism and a new medication regime after 1948, until the colony was disbanded in 1957. Allow at least ninety minutes to explore the fortifications and the old town. Part of the old market street has been restored, the renovated shops now house an interesting museum.

Whitewashed walls of mountainous Kritsá

Inland to Kritsá

Inland from Ágios Nikólaos are three attractions that fill an enjoyable morning or afternoon of sightseeing. Head out towards the village of Kritsá 12km (7 miles) from town. Before you reach the village itself you'll find a beautiful Byzantine chapel on the right. **Panagía Kerá** ⓰ (https://agiosnikolaoscrete.com/religion/panagia-kera; free) was built in the 13th century and decorated with superb frescoes of the 14th and 15th centuries. You'll need time, and the guide booklet on sale, to take in every detail of the interior. Although many frescoes are damaged or uncleaned, existing highlights include a 'Presentation of the Virgin' and 'Last Supper' in the vault of the main nave, and the 'Water of Proof' in the south aisle.

Resume your journey toward Kritsá, but don't visit the village just yet. Instead, follow signs 4km (2.5 miles) along a side road to **Lató** (free access). It's not an official site, rather the remains of a

Dorian city (seventh to third centuries BC) scattered around two scrub-covered hilltops to the north.

Finally, head into **Kritsá** for some well-earned refreshments and rest. This 'traditional' village is perhaps overly touristy for some, but it is still very much lived-in and extremely well kept with brilliant-whitewashed walls accented by colourful window frames and potted plants. Good tavernas can be found near the old village square – distinguished by its huge plane tree. Famed for its carpet weaving and textiles, you'll also see them hanging from walls and shop doorways in the narrow streets.

Lasíthi Plateau and the Dikti Mountain

The Lasíthi Plateau

If Kritsá is a good example of a hill-village 'rescued' by tourism, others have seen their rural economy collapse since the 1970s. Travelling inland toward the towering peaks of the **Díkti Mountains** brings you to a region that was isolated from the rest of Crete, except by horse or donkey travel, until well after World War II. Improved access to the **Lasíthi Plateau** ⓱ (Oropédio Lasithíou) ironically just accelerated the depopulation.

Two main roads climb up to 850m (2,800ft) altitude. From the New Road above Mália you head through the tiny settlements of **Krási**, with an ancient plane tree gracing the main square, and

Kerá, where you can visit fourteenth-century **Panagía Kardiotíssis** – Our Lady of the Heart (free) before proceeding through the dramatic **Séli Ambélou Pass** with its ruined stone windmills.

Or ascend from Neápoli on a longer road not used by tour coaches, through the little oases of **Exo** and **Mésa Potámi**, for a panoramic initial view of the plain and the impressive **Psarí Madára** peak (2,148m/7,047ft) beyond.

A single road circles the plain, linking all the small communities, though you'll find many of their houses derelict or rented by Romani people, and their shops shuttered since the flight down the mountain. What agricultural activity that persists is often much delayed by heavy spring rains in the last few years while awaiting for the valley floor to drain. Potatoes and grain grow on the plateau, with sheep grazing the stubble; orchards (especially apples and cherries) and vines are cultivated on the surrounding slopes. The famous windmills, which used to pump up water in late spring, have now mostly vanished; just a few at the north edge of the plateau are left spinning idly for show, their pistons disconnected and storage tanks empty.

On the southern edge of the plain, 1km (0.5 miles) above **Psyhró** village where powerful springs nourish a plane tree, yawns the large **Dictean Cave** (Diktéon Andron; temporarily closed at time of writing; charge), said to be the birthplace of Zeus. Ancient votive offerings left in the cave confirm that it was revered during Minoan times. It is a 15-minute walk (or expensive mule ride) from the parking lot. From the entrance, the cave drops precipitously 65m (215ft) into the cavern, which can get very crowded. Try to spot the monstrous face of Kronos, eating his new offspring Zeus, and the small nipple-shaped stalagmites on which the infant god is said to have suckled.

East to Sitía

Heading east from Ágios Nikólaos, the new road along the northern coast is still in the throes of construction and once finished, will significantly reduce travel time – currently 1.5 hours. Follow the gulf initially south to **Ístro** where there is a garland of beaches (best of these being **Voúlisma**), and then east to one of the major open ancient sites locally – **Gourniá** ⓲, 18km (11 miles) from Ágios Nikólaos (https://gournia.org; charge). Myriad stone walls – foundations for multi-storeyed homes – linked by cobbled streets blanket the hillside. Here, more than at any other Minoan site, it is possible to envision ordinary people going about their daily business. You can also explore the marketplace and workshops of the artisans.

The palace sat at the top of the hill, its west court housing a sacrificial slab and storerooms for ritual liquids and libations as seen in other Minoan palaces. Gourniá was a large city, stretching all the way down to the coast where it had an important and busy port. However, much remains to be uncovered. The best overview of Gourniá – excavated by American Harriet Boyd Hawkes in the early 1900s – is from the main road as it rises beyond the archeological site.

From Gourniá the Old National Road traces a tortuous course via sleepy hill-villages towards Sitía. The one spot of note actually on the coast, down one of two side roads, is **Móhlos** ⓳, now an easygoing resort on a cape despite lacking a beach, but during Minoan times an important site. The Minoan settlement sits on a small islet a mere 150m (480ft) offshore – you can take a small boat (charge – find one when you get there) or swim across to reach it – although it was connected to the mainland three thousand years ago. A little way offshore to the west is **Psíra**, for which you will definitely need boat transportation to visit the Minoan port town.

Eventually the northern road drops into **Sitía** ⓴, a bustling port town of about nine thousand people – including students at the local geological school and police academy, who keep the waterfront bars and *ouzerís* lively all year.

A Minoan settlement at **Petrás**, an open site (free) that lies 1km (0.5 miles) to the east, but the Venetians chose this hillside location, building a fortress – the **Kazárma** – on its highest point (+30 2843 027 140;

Sitía's waterfront

charge). Unfortunately, the Turks destroyed the Venetian domestic buildings when they took the town but a network of narrow lanes and stone steps spill down to a waterfront promenade, and these have delightful architectural and lifestyle details to discover. Sitía also has a pleasing **Archaeological Museum** (https://archaeologicalmuseums.gr/en/museum/5df34af3deca5e2d79e8c15b/archaeological-museum-of-siteia; charge) displaying finds mostly from Zákros, in particular a large collection of painted *lárnakes* (clay burial chambers), as well as a ceramic wine press and *souvláki* grill. You'll find it just south of the town centre.

Toploú to Zákros

Sitía is the gateway to the far east of Crete. Now sparsely populated, with most villages located inland and subsisting on olives and grapes, this region conceals important Minoan sites suggesting that many people lived here three thousand years ago. For those who want to explore the area there's plenty of accommodation around Palékastro and Káto Zákros. Surprisingly, in this remote part of the island a procession of tour buses arrives every day from Ágios Nikólaos and beyond.

Many of these are headed for one of Crete's most influential religious institutions, **Moní Toploú** ㉑ (Toploú Monastery; https://imis.gr/el/-7039; charge), an oasis in an otherwise rather bleak landscape, owned almost entirely by the Orthodox Church. Founded in the fourteenth century, the monastery was built for contemplation, but also for protection against outside threats. Toploú is a Turkish word meaning 'with cannon' – the more correct title for the monastery is Kyriá Akrotirianí – indicating that the abbots were no timorous recluses. Its walls suggest more a fortress than a religious refuge – though even these were not enough to protect it from being sacked by pirates in 1498. The monastery played a signal role in Cretan uprisings against the Turks – twelve monks were hanged in 1821 – and more recently against the Germans in World War II when it was a safe-house for British soldiers and native partisans. The abbot and several monks were shot in reprisal before the war's end.

Moní Toploú

The monastery church and museum shelters many treasures, foremost among them the intricate 18th-century icon by Ioannis Kornaros, with 61 miniature scenes based on the Orthodox prayer 'Lord, Thou Art Great'; at its top is a finely wrought Holy Trinity, framed rather bizarrely by zodiacal signs. There are also two galleries of strange and rare engravings, plus illuminated gospels. Sadly, most of the monastery, other than the courtyard, is now off-limits. In the extensive gift shop, you can buy reproductions of the icon or olive oil produced from the monks' own groves. September 26 is the monastery's celebration day, attracting many pilgrims to the site.

> **NOTES**
>
> Zákros, the last Minoan settlement to be excavated (in the 1960s), revealed a wealth of undisturbed artefacts. Tools and ceremonial objects were found just where they were dropped at the time of the great cataclysm, along with the crystal rhyton on view in the Iráklio Museum and a chest containing hundreds of clay tablets inscribed with Linear A script. Archeologists even discovered an urn with olives preserved through the millennia.

Northeast of Toploú awaits one of Crete's natural wonders. Amid arid scenery, a grove of verdant date palms appears, with beyond a swathe of blond sand lapped by azure waters. This is **Váï** ㉒, extremely beautiful and correspondingly popular at peak season, when it's absolutely packed. The palms are claimed to have grown from pips spat out by Arab pirates, though the less romantic truth is that they're an indigenous variety *(Phoenix theophrastii)* that have been present here for millennia. If Váï is 'full', retire instead to three less crowded sandy coves 3km (2 miles) north at **Itanos** – there are date palms here too at the southerly cove.

From both Váï and Toploú, roads converge on modern **Palékastro** village, with the Minoan site of Rousolakkos nearby (still being excavated, free access), overlooking Hióna beach, the

The ruins of the Palace of Zákros

ancient port. This is separated by a headland from superior **Koureménos** ㉓ beach with its windsurfing facilities.

South from Palékastro, the narrower road shies away from the coast, threading villages that are trailheads for great hikes, including through two gorges: the **Hohlahiés canyon**, ending at isolated Karoúmes beach, and the more famous **Zákros Gorge** (better known as the **Valley of the Dead**). Either take about ninety minutes going downhill (two hours up), with year-round drinking water in the 'Deads' Gorge' (as it's signposted locally). Your reward, at the bottom of Zákros, is a Minoan palace and another long beach with several tavernas.

The **Palace of Zákros** ㉔ (https://ancient-greece.org/archaeology/zakros; charge) sits just behind this strand on flat ground, with its associated town flanking it on the hillside. With its large port, Zákros was well situated for trade with Egypt and Syria. Building began around 1900BC, though these remains are now invisible owing to subsidence. The exposed, second palace was completed *c.*1600BC, but the cataclysm of 1450BC saw a sudden abandonment of the city; it was never resettled.

The **west wing** of the palace was mostly devoted to cult practices, with workshops in the south. The **north wing** housed the royal entourage and the main kitchen, while the east was reserved for the royal apartments. Archeologists discovered treasures in many of these rooms.

One unique aspect of Zákros is the east wing's water feature, behind the royal apartments. The **cistern hall** contains a circular cistern, still full of water, now inhabited by Caspian pond terrapins. Nearby, the ceremonial 'built fountain' has steps descending to a small, square pool.

The southeastern coast

At **Xérokambos**, the next shoreline settlement beyond Káto Zákros, the road turns inland to arrive dramatically at upland **Zíros** village; the coast below is either inaccessible by car or unrewarding if you do get to it. At Zíros you might prefer to stay inland, meeting the main road south from Sitía just past **Etiá** ㉕, a Venetian-founded village, now abandoned, with a rare and superbly restored Venetian manor-house (De Mezzo Mansion; charge) containing a worthwhile display on life in Venetian Crete.

However you travel, the next reasonable halting-point is **Makrý Gialós** ㉖, a low-key if straggly resort with an equally long, gently shelving beach and portside tavernas. From here west the coast is more populated, with pine trees and small sandy bays (the most scenic of these **Agía Fotiá** and **Ahliá**) en route to Ierápetra, also reachable by a direct road across the narrowest point of Crete from near Gourniá.

NOTES

From Ierápetra's jetty you can take a trip to Hrissí (Gaïdouro) islet, some 7 nautical miles offshore but plainly visible on the horizon. This nearly flat islet is covered in rare junipers and has at least two white-sand beaches. In season it's possible to eat lunch in the harbour's tavern. Excursion boats leave in the summer every half hour from 10.30am until 12pm (charge), returning from Hrissí in the afternoon.

The mosque in Ierápetra, Europe's southernmost town

Ierápetra ㉗ is the fourth-largest settlement on Crete and claims to be the southernmost town in Europe. As ancient Ierapytna, it was the last Cretan city to fall to the Romans, who used it as a base for their conquest of Egypt. Today Ierápetra is a thriving agricultural-supply centre, enveloped in ranks of plastic greenhouses, with a resort tacked on to the east almost as an afterthought. The limited list of conventional tourist attractions in the small old quarter comprises a tiny Venetian castle (Kales Fortress; https://ierapetra.gr/index.php/en/history-culture/byzantine-venetian-period/265-venetian-fortress-kales; free), an eighteenth-century mosque (free) with truncated minaret, and a small archeological 'collection' (+30 28420 28721; charge) inside a former Koranic school.

West of Ierápetra, the greenhouses have mostly vanished by the time you reach **Mýrtos** ㉘, 16km (10 miles) along, a laid-back, slightly 'alternative' resort just beyond the Minoan sites of Foúrnou Korýfi and Pýrgos. Despite German destruction in late 1943 as reprisal for resistance activity, it's a cheerful, welcoming place, almost a proper town, with a long beach and the Nikos Kazantzakis Museum (https://kazantzaki.gr/en; charge). The author of *Zorba the Greek* was born in Iráklio in 1885. If for any reason you don't like

Mýrtos, continue 5km (3 miles) west to **Tértsa**, another long beach with the summits of the Díkti range visible overhead. With a car, make the trip west and inland (33km/21 miles) to **Áno Viánnos** ㉙, a surprisingly large village in the Díkti foothills overlooking a fertile plain. The big attraction here is a tiny 14th-century **Agía Pelagía** church up the hill (well signposted, always open), with idiosyncratic frescoes from the life of Christ. From here it's easy to continue on into Iráklio district.

Western Crete

Highlights

- **South of Réthymno**, see page 79
- **The south coast**, see page 81
- **Réthymno to Haniá**, see page 83
- **Haniá**, see page 85
- **West of Haniá**, see page 88
- **The White Mountains and the Samariá Gorge**, see page 90

Western Crete offers a diverse range of attractions: two delightful towns on the north coast, unspoiled mountains where you can hike or experience Cretan rural life and tiny south-coast villages accessible only on foot or by boat. This area is less densely populated than Iráklio district and has more rainfall, making it lushly vegetated. These contrasts make it a fascinating part of the island to spend a vacation.

Réthymno ㉚ lies 75km (50 miles) west of Iráklio, one hour away along the New National Road. The site has been settled since Minoan times, with Dorian, Greek and Roman remains underlying the present town. Venetian rule spawned many of the architectural gems here, although evidence of the Ottoman period also abounds. Réthymno suffered many attacks and sackings over the centuries. Much of the town was badly damaged in the battle for Crete during World War II, although the old quarter survived. Today, a modern tourist district extends to the east, taking advantage of the long sandy bay, but this has not spoilt the old town, a delightful place to stroll.

Réthymno has also been the intellectual centre of Crete throughout the ages, home to the island's most esteemed university. Annually in July the town attracts artists from across Greece for its Renaissance Festival.

The old town occupies a strategic nub of land jutting out from the long, flat coastline. A huge fortress – the **Fortezza** (+30 28310 28210; charge) – dominates the site, its walls rising high above the streets on the northwestern point. This is considered to be the largest fortification ever built by the Venetians, who completed the task in 1580. The finest views of the walls are from the waterfront promenade outside, from where you can appreciate its grand scale.

The Fortezza at Réthymno

Once inside, it is easy to imagine a large garrison stationed here, with the ruins of barracks and arsenals scattered everywhere. Right at the heart of it is the restored, 1647-built **Mosque of Ibrahim Han**, the largest domed structure in Greece, now hosting concerts or art exhibits. Despite its strength and dominant position, Ottoman forces made surprisingly light work of taking the fortress in 1646 – they simply landed elsewhere on the coast and invaded the town from the land.

Walking downhill from the fortress gate brings you to the enchanting **Venetian inner harbour**, now a haven for small fishing craft and excursion boats, guarded by a nineteenth-century lighthouse at the end of the stone jetty. Unfortunately, the harbour cafés, where Ottoman Cretans used to socialise over coffee and shared *nargilédes* (hubble-bubbles), have now become somewhat touristy tavernas.

NOTES

The Renaissance Festival in Rethymno (https://rfr.gr), an annual event held in late summer, is a vibrant celebration of the town's Venetian past. Set against the atmospheric backdrop of the Fortezza and the old town's cobbled streets, expect theatrical performances, music concerts, art exhibitions, and traditional Cretan dance, all inspired by the sixteenth and seventeenth centuries. Locals and visitors alike are transported back in time through colourful parades, period costumes, and open-air events that showcase Réthymno's rich cultural heritage and enduring creative spirit.

Behind the old harbour the maze of narrow, mostly pedestrianised streets, ideal for strolling, forms the core of the old quarter. The most obvious sight will be shopping opportunities at eye level: craft and jewellery stores create tempting displays, and cotton clothing is swathed across every wall.

Be sure to look behind the touristy merchandise to see Venetian stone lintels above, glimpse ornate Ottoman *kióskia* (enclosed wooden balconies) or entire housefronts draped in bougainvillaea. At night the streets come alive with shoppers and revellers, and excellent restaurants occupy some of the old buildings.

If you exit the harbour from the southwest, you cross busy Arkadíou towards the **Venetian Loggia**, built in 1600. It has been rescued from years of dereliction, now housing an upmarket gallery where you can buy excellent copies of museum pieces. Walk down Paleológou to find the still-flowing **Rimondi Fountain**. Built in the 1620s, its lion-head spouts have taken on an aged patina and it looks strangely out of place in this bustling square.

From here the principal shopping street, Ethnikís Antistáseos, leads south. Turn right onto Vernárdou where you will immediately find the **Nerantzés Mosque** (Tzamí ton Nerantzión), a converted Venetian church – something obvious from the north portal – now used as a conservatory and concert hall. Beyond this the **Historical and Folklore Museum** (Rethimno 74131; https://rethymno.gr/en/city/historical-museum/historical-museum.html; charge), in a fine old Venetian mansion, provides an evocative glimpse of bygone Crete. The upstairs galleries feature embroidery, weavings, farm and kitchen implements and ceramics. Situated on the same street is also the **Museum of Contemporary Art of Crete** (Himaras 5; https://cca.gr; charge). The permanent exhibition showcases works from contemporary Greek artists.

Ethnikís Antistáseos soon ends at the **Porta Goura**; this stone gateway, all that remains of the original town walls, separates the old quarter from the traffic-filled twenty-first century just beyond. Across the busy boulevard is the tempting shade of the **Municipal Gardens**, formerly a Muslim cemetery. Within ten minutes' walk of the Gardens is the recently relocated **Archaeological Museum** (Saint Francis Church; Saint Francis 4; https://archmuseumreth.gr; charge) displaying late Minoan and Roman finds including clay sarcophagi painted with stylised animals.

NOTES

There are several other fountains, now dry and inscribed with elegant Ottoman calligraphy, scattered across town. The easiest to find are alongside the multi-domed Kara Pasha Mosque and on the corner of Smýrnis and Koronéou, below the Fortezza.

South of Réthymno

The area south of Réthymno is well worth exploring by car, but its major attraction can be visited by public or tour bus. **Moní Arkadíou** 31 (Arkádi Monastery; https://arkadimonastery.gr; charge – book tickets online) lies in the Psiloritis foothills some 23km (14 miles) south-east of Réthymno. It was founded in the Byzantine era, although its present buildings date from the late sixteenth century and is revered by Cretans as a nationalist shrine.

Souvenirs for sale in Réthymno's old town

In 1866 the Orthodox islanders rebelled yet once more against Ottoman rule. As the attempt failed, hundreds of partisans sought sanctuary in the compound. The Muslims demanded their surrender and, when Abbot Gavriíl (Gabriel) refused, they besieged the monastery.

On 9 November the attackers breached the outer walls to find the Greeks barricaded in a wine depot, where they had also stored their gunpowder. As the Ottoman forces made their way toward this last refuge, the abbot ordered the explosives to be fired. The resulting blast killed hundreds of defenders and attackers, giving real meaning to the battle cry of Crete – 'freedom or death'.

Today, the monastery is a much more peaceful place, although the fateful storeroom remains a charred shell. The Venetian-style church gracing the middle of the compound is one of the most beautiful on

Crete. Its façade of yellow sandstone is richly carved with a fine belfry, and mock Corinthian columns dignify each of the twin entranceways.

From **Moní Arkadíou**, it is only about six kilometres east to the recently inaugurated **Museum of Ancient Eleutherna** (https://mae.uoc.gr; charge). The collection consists of three rooms. Room A presents the everyday life in ancient Eleutherna. Room B and C show respectively the religious practices and burial customs of the site's community from the Iron Age to the Byzantine era.

Southeast of Réthymno lie two valleys leading towards the far coast. The **Amári Valley** ㉜ is the more easterly and the more exciting, with traditional rural landscapes to explore and dramatic views of Psilorítis as a backdrop. You'll need a car or mountain bike, as public buses or tours up here don't operate, and accommodation scarce. The main valley loop-road leads through small villages, many graced with fine old, frescoed churches, and all with memorials commemorating the 1944 German reprisals exacted for resistance operations.

At **Thrónos**, the eleventh-century **Panagía chapel** has superb, later frescoes – the shop next door keeps the key (no formal charge, but a tip is expected). The adjacent hamlet of **Kalógeros** is home to the small **Theológos chapel**, with more fourteenth-century frescoes. **Monastiráki**, southeast of here, offers two more churches: tiny **Aï Geórgi**, at the top of the village, with a fine image of the Panagía Platytéra, and Venetian-style **Arhángelos** (the key can be obtained from the café opposite) retains a fresco of the Dormition. East from here, **Platánia** has another Panagía chapel (key from nearby café) with a vivid, nearly complete cycle of frescoes, some unusual – note the rarely shown Angel Gabriel, and St George with a right earring in the Byzantine manner. Going instead anticlockwise from Thrónos, **Méronas** offers the **Metamórfosi chapel** by the school, with well-preserved scenes of St Stephen and the Transfiguration, but the central village church of **Panagía**, with the most complete fresco cycle in the valley, is only rarely opened by the priest.

The second valley to the west leads up to the little hill-town of **Spíli**. Stop to sample the central **Venetian fountain** – a series of thirty kitsch-modern lion-heads spouting crystal clear, cool water from Mt Kédros overhead – before exploring the backstreets. The **Folk Museum of Spili** (free), within a short walk of the fountain, is also worth a visit. The small exhibition contains tools that used to be owned by the members of the local community and gives an idea of how a traditional Cretan house would have looked.

Moní Arkadíou, a national Cretan shrine

The south coast

Beyond Spíli the main road heads east towards Agía Galíni (see page 57), but turn right 6km (4 miles) before Spíli to pass through the dramatic **Kourtaliótiko Gorge** en route to Plakiás and Préveli Monastery on the south coast.

Moní Préveli ㉝ (Préveli Monastery; https://preveli.org; charge) is a remote religious community and, like most others, was involved in partisan activities during Crete's struggles for freedom. The fathers helped many Allied prisoners to escape in World War II, while an earlier monastery (Káto Préveli – you pass the evocative but fenced-off ruins en route) was sacked in 1821. Newer Préveli dates from the seventeenth century and was the richest religious house in Crete during the Ottoman era. Its church contains a splendid iconostasis, considered the best on the island, while in the small treasury museum a gold and diamond crucifix purportedly contains a piece of the True Cross.

Below the monastery, a steep track descends to the car park for '**Palm Beach**', a sandy, stream-fed cove from which the World War II evacuations took place.

In the other direction, west along the coast, minor roads lead to **Plakiás** ❸❹ and beyond. Plakiás is a burgeoning resort situated along a crescent-shaped bay, though better beaches flank it at **Damnóni** and **Ammoúdi** to the east, and **Soúda** on the west.

West over the border in Haniá district, the walls of **Frangokástello** ❸❺ can be seen rising behind a sandy beach. This dramatic 14th-century fortress is now just an empty shell – like a set for a film about the French Foreign Legion. The Venetians built it not only to ward off pirates but to intimidate Cretan fighters in the mountains behind. During Ottoman rule Frangokástello was the scene of many critical events, including the capture of the rebel Daskalogiannis in 1770 and the massacre of seven hundred Cretans in 1828.

This secondary coast road ends at Komitádes, just beyond which stands **Hóra Sfakíón** ❸❻, a little port resort that was the main

Small waterfalls flowing at Kourtaliótiko Gorge

MISTS OR MYSTERIES?

Every year in mid-May local people living near Frangokástello say that they can see the spirits of the dead rebels from 1828 marching around the base of the castle. These *drosoulítes* or 'dewy ones' rise from the morning mists, and meteorologists assure us that they are simply a form of weather phenomena, not phantasms.

Allied evacuation point after the Battle of Crete in 1941; a memorial commemorates the event. The road veers inland towards **Anópoli**, and coastal points west of Hóra can only be reached by boat or on foot. Boats pick hikers up from the base of the Samariá Gorge, and at busy times rows of tour buses await here to whisk them away. You can take boat trips to inhabited **Gávdos** islet, the most southern territory in Europe, or to nearby **Loutró**, a picturesque village with no vehicular access; alternatively, you can hike west along the E4 trail to Loutró, Anópoli and many points beyond.

From Komitádes, the main road follows the spectacular **Imbros Gorge** ㊲, with its rich flora and fauna. This gorge is easier than the nearby Samariá, and you can descend it (takes 2.5 hrs approximately) by leaving your car at the village of Ímbros. **Komitádes** marks the bottom, where you can take an afternoon bus or taxi back to your start point.

Réthymno to Haniá

The coastline between Réthymno and Haniá has its share of resorts, although sandy coves are not the rule. An exception is **Georgioúpoli** ㊳, with a long, sandy beach demarcated by a river on the west. Its best feature, however, is nearby **Lake Kourná**, the only freshwater lake in Crete, surprisingly large, with idyllic swimming and pedalos or kayaks to rent.

Northeast from here, via the characterful inland village of **Vámos, Kalýves** and **Almyrída** are the busiest spots. All roads emerge at **Soúda Bay**, home of Crete's largest port and one of the Mediterranean's best deepwater anchorages. It is the port for Haniá, with ferry services to Piraeus, while the Greek Navy shares a large base here with NATO. The **British Commonwealth War cemetery** can be found at the head of the bay.

Lake Kourná with White Mountains in background

The **Akrotíri Peninsula** 39 flanks Soúda on the north. Here you'll find Haniá's airport, several small villages and beaches, plus three important monasteries. Seventeenth-century **Agía Triáda** is today largely a museum, the most imposing item its Venetian façade, with a small shop selling monastic wine and olive oil. More isolated **Gouvernétou Monastery** – Our Lady of the Angels-4km (2.5 miles) north is a functioning monastery not open to non-Orthodox, but it marks the start of the strenous, two-hour (round trip) hike down to the evocative remains of **Katholikó**, Crete's first and oldest monastery, founded in the 11th century by St John the Hermit. Set on the side of a rocky ravine, it was abandoned during the seventeenth century in response to pirate raids in favour of Gouvernétou.

As you head towards Haniá, stop at the **tombs of Eleftherios Venizelos** (1864–1936) (free), Crete's greatest statesman, and of his son Sophokles. On this spot, on the orders of Eleftherios Venizelos, the Greek flag was raised in 1897 in defiance of ongoing negotiations amongst the major European powers about the fate of Crete. There are wonderful views across the bay to Haniá, and an adjacent bar from which to enjoy them.

Haniá

The capital of Crete from 1845 until 1971, **Haniá** ⓴ remains the island's second-largest settlement, and despite extensive modern development at the outskirts, remains an immediately likeable place, currently more prosperous than Iráklio, and one of the few cities where Greeks from elsewhere choose to live. At its heart is a delightful old town replete with Venetian and Ottoman buildings and full of cosmopolitan atmosphere, considered to be one of the most beautiful in the whole of Greece.

The **Venetian harbour** attracts visitors and locals alike. It is huge by comparison with Réthymno's, with outer and inner sections. The waterfront is lined with beautiful medieval buildings and numerous cafés and tavernas, an evening lodestar of attraction. The faded stucco of the harbour buildings takes on a delicate rosy hue as night falls, contrasting with the deep blue sky.

The **Firkás bastion** at the northwest corner of the outer harbour is a Venetian ramparts housing the **Maritime Museum of Crete** Ⓐ (Naftikó Mousío; mar-mus-crete.gr; charge), founded to house and preserve Cretan maritime traditions, displaying shells, model ships, maps and naval paraphernalia. Walk through the archway beyond the museum entrance for views east across the harbour from the bastion. Nearby on Theotokopoúlou, the Venetian church of San Salvatore shelters the well-designed **Byzantine and Post-Byzantine Collection** Ⓑ (https://archaeologicalmuseums.gr/en/museum/5df34af3deca5e2d79e8c160/byzantine-and-post-byzantine-collection-of-chania; charge), with icons of the Cretan School, jewellery, coins, a floor mosaic and fresco fragments rescued from nearby country chapels.

If you walk down to the sea from here, you can follow partly pedestrianised Pireós inland along the finest surviving section of the old city walls, ending at the massive **Skhiávo bastion** Ⓒ. Staying instead by the sea leads to Neahóra, with its beach and tavernas.

Across the harbour from the Maritime Museum you'll see the impressive buttressed dome of the **Giáli Tzamí** Ⓓ (Shore Mosque; free), the first mosque built by the Ottomans in 1645. Beyond the mosque leads to the inner harbour, with the remains of large Venetian **arsenália** (ship repair yards) – originally seventeen lined the water's edge. You can then continue out along the pier to the nineteenth-century lighthouse at the harbour mouth.

The old quarters extend behind the harbour: narrow alleyways with a mélange of Venetian and Ottoman buildings, a canvas of faded terracotta and ochre stucco dressed with restaurant signs or wares for sale. The shopping here is the most sophisticated on the island, a legacy of Haniá's days as a bohemian hangout in the 1960s.

Although the streets all seem to run together, there are four recognised sections of the old town. **Tophanás** ('Cannon Hall' in Turkish) behind the Naval Museum, was the Ottoman administrative quarter. Theotokopoúlou, lined with fine Venetian mansions and fashionable cafés, bounds it to the west. At the corner of Zambelíou and Móskhon stands the **Renieri Gate**, built in 1608.

Evraïkí, to the southeast, was the Jewish Quarter during Venetian times. Its small houses awash with pastel hues offer the most shopping and eating possibilities. A synagogue, **Etz Hayyim** Ⓔ, has been restored for visits (https://etz-hayyim-hania.org; charge), although all of Haniá Jews were deported by the Germans. **Kastélli**, east of the Shore Mosque, was the centre of the Venetian city – as the name suggests there was an older castle here, rendered obsolete when Haniá expanded during the sixteenth century. You'll see a Venetian arcade at the bottom of

Agíou Márkou. Kastélli was also the site of Minoan, Greek and Roman Kydonia, the ancient town, partly exposed on Kanevárou.

The easternmost old quarter is **Splántzia**, characterised by whitewashed churches and cobbled alleyways. Platía 1821 forms the core of this neighbourhood, which has more authentic daily life than any other part of old Haniá.

The **Archaeological Museum** of Chania F (www-amch-gr; charge – advisable to book tickets ahead online) has recently moved to a new location in an iconic building in the historic suburb of Chalepa. The collection spans all eras but is strongest on painted Minoan *larnakes* (clay coffins), Roman statuettes, and Hellenistic mosaics.

Nearby is the **Folklore Museum "Cretan House"** G (https://chaniatourism.gr/museum/folklore-museum-of-chania-cretan-house; charge), tucked away in a tiny square alongside the Roman Catholic church of the Assumption, essentially an old house crammed with an array of antiques and textiles; reproductions of old embroidery are available to purchase.

Skrydlóf H (Leather Street), with its mix of traditional goods and trashy souvenirs, heads off Halídon towards the **Agorá**, or covered market, one of Crete's shopping highlights.

Sunset over Haniá's lighthouse

NOTES

The two islands off Gramvoúsa Peninsula both take its name – Iméri (tame) and Ágria (wild) Gramvoúsa.

Al Hammam Traditional Baths ❶ (https://alhammam.gr; charge), Tucked away in Chania's atmospheric old Turkish Quarter, Al Hammam offers a serene escape within a beautifully restored seventeenth-century Ottoman bathhouse. Unwind with traditional steam rituals, exfoliating scrubs, and massages in a setting that blends historic charm with modern wellness.

West of Haniá

As there are few good beaches near Haniá, many people stay in resorts to the west and simply travel in for the day. **Plataniás** is an excellent the coastal resort with a lively atmosphere, as are **Agía Marína** and quieter **Geráni**. Just 15 kilometres (about 25 minutes' drive) inland from Plataniás lies the village of **Vouves**, home to one of the world's oldest living olive trees – believed to be over four thousand years old. Visiting this ancient botanical marvel offers a rare chance to connect with the island's deep-rooted agricultural heritage. The gnarled trunk of the tree, sculpted by centuries of wind and weather, is a natural monument of resilience, and next to it, the small **Olive Tree Museum** (free) provides fascinating insight into traditional Cretan olive cultivation

Continuing west, **Máleme** is the furthest resort proper; after this, accommodation can be found only in private rooms or small local hotels. The town has a sad legacy, as it was the airfield here (still active) that German paratroopers first seized in 1941, signalling the start of the battle for Crete. Casualties were high for these pioneers, and the **German war cemetery** above the airfield holds the graves of more than four thousand young men.

Beyond Máleme, the rugged peninsulas of **Rodopoú** and **Gramvoúsa**, jut out from the northern coast, offer plenty of excursions (best to the Goniá Monastery, and Ágios Ioánnis shrine, on Rodopoú, or the lagoon of Bálos on Gramvoúsa). They bracket the port town of **Kíssamos** 41 (aka Kastélli), unremarkable except for its superb **Archaeological Museum** (http://odysseus.culture.gr/h/1/gh151.jsp?obj_id=3465; charge), strongest on Roman/Hellenistic Kissamos, with a brilliant villa mosaic of 'The Seasons' upstairs. Beyond Kíssamos, the broad sandy beach at **Falásarna**, complete with ancient town, and the beautiful lagoon at **Elafónisos** attract numerous day-trippers.

The route from Máleme to Paleóhora on the south coast provides a microcosm of what western Crete is all about. From the wide coastal plain, you climb, then drop, through small villages,

Picturesque lane in Haniá's old town

the biggest – **Kándanos** – rebuilt after a wartime atrocity and sporting several unlocked, frescoed chapels. Your destination, **Paleohóra** ⓬42, is a laid-back town with a crumbled Venetian fort and two beaches – Gialiskári (pebbles) and Pahiá Ammos (long and sandy) embracing it. A partly-pedestrianised main street offers every diversion after dark. This is also the end of the line for the south-coast ferries – you can head east towards Hóra Sfakíon.

A different road from Kándanos leads to **Soúgia** 43, an even more relaxed, smaller resort with a huge sand-and-pebble beach (naturists throng the far end) and a variety of walking possibilities, including the hour-plus hike west to **ancient Lissós** through a spectacular gorge.

Walking the Samariá Gorge

The White Mountains and the Samariá Gorge

The **White Mountains** 44 (Lefká Óri), the island's highest range, with several peaks exceeding 2,000m (5,600ft), dominate western Crete. There are almost no villages on its south flank because the mountains rise so abruptly from the Libyan Sea. This is an unforgiving landscape, rugged and stunningly beautiful, with narrow valleys between limestone peaks that wear a mantle of snow until May. Yet these mountains host one of Crete's most impressive, popular and enjoyable excursions – the 16km (10-mile) walk down the famous **Samariá Gorge** ㊺ (https://samaria.gr; charge; entrances at Xylóskala and Agía Rouméli). Starting at an elevation of 1,240m (4,068ft), the gorge is the longest in Europe, swollen with meltwater during winter. Only during summer, when the torrent shrinks to a trickle, are people allowed to follow its path. Ancient cypress trees, rare orchids and soaring birds of prey are the overwhelming attractions.

NOTES

The Samariá Gorge is one of the few places where you might catch a glimpse of the elusive Cretan wild goat known as the *agrími* or *krí-krí*. Built like an ibex, with long curving adult horns, it is sometimes spotted leaping between crags in the White Mountains.

Despite the strenuous nature of the trek – don't set out without sturdy footwear, a hat, sunscreen and a full water bottle – you'll share the narrow pathway with hundreds of other intrepid tourists, which adds to the camaraderie, but can spoil the atmosphere if you hoped for solitude. However early you start, you're unlikely to beat the crowds. Most people pay for an excursion that provides a bus ride to the head of the gorge at **Xylóskala** (wooden staircase) and boat transfer from Agía Rouméli, at the southern end, to Hóra Sfakión where you rejoin the bus. If you travel independently, you can take a bus from Haniá to Omalós, just before Xylóskala, and then a boat east to Hóra Sfakión, or west to Soúgia or Paleohóra.

The National Park containing the gorge opens daily at 6am from May to mid-October; after 3pm the main section is closed. Park wardens sell you a ticket, to be surrendered at the other end to ensure that no one is left stranded in the gorge. The descent begins at Xylóskala, in reality, a steeply descending path with wooden balustrades for much of the way. With wall-like **Mt Gíngilos** towering above, the stone path drops sharply away in a series of switchbacks, falling 1,000m (3,300ft) in the first 3km (2 miles).

The route becomes less steep once you reach the **Chapel of Ágios Nikólaos**, 4km (2.5 miles) in, where there is a picnic area. Springtime freshwater pools are inviting, but swimming is strictly forbidden. The abandoned village of **Samariá**, with its 14th-century **Church of Osía María** (Mary the Anointed of Egypt), marks the halfway point. People lived here until 1962; now there's only a warden's post and first-aid station. Beyond looms the gorge's narrowest, most memorable point, the **Siderespórtes** (Iron Gates), only 3.5m (11ft) wide but 300m (1,000ft) high. Beyond this, the gorge opens up as it approaches the sea and is much less striking.

The White Mountains

The final stretch is perhaps the most gruelling as you walk along the shadeless riverbed, but at **Agía Rouméli** 46 you'll be able to enjoy an extremely welcome drink or meal.

Excursion to Santoríni

Highlights

- **Firá**, see page 93
- **Ía**, see page 94
- **Pýrgos**, Profítis Ilías and Akrotíri, see page 95

Although Crete is interesting and varied, you may want to spend a day or two exploring a different Greek island. **Santoríni** (aka **Thíra**) is the most popular and accessible at just a couple of hours by fast catamaran from Iráklio. Day trips are offered in every resort.

Arriving by sea allows gradual comprehension of the stunning topography unfolding before you, for Santoríni frames the largest submerged volcanic caldera on earth. A massive eruption of this volcano around 1500BC carried the whole interior of the island high into the atmosphere as ash, changing the climate of the earth for years afterwards. In place of land came water, surging in to fill the 11km (7-mile) -long void and causing massive tidal waves around the Aegean. What remains today is the outer rim of the original circular island. Sheer cliffs up to 300m (980ft) high bound the caldera, and a number of whitewashed settlements nestle along their crests.

Firá

The island capital is **Firá**, perched atop high cliffs in the centre of the long interior curve. Its buildings tumble towards the water below, giving stunning views. A narrow, cobbled trail of 587 steps leads from the town to the small port below, now the domain of a fleet of donkeys that wait to carry cruise-ship passengers into

Santoríni's capital, Firá

town. There is also a quicker cable car that whisks you up from sea level in a couple of minutes. Most commercial ferries arrive at **Athiniós** port, south along the coast.

Firá's narrow, traffic-free alleys make up a shopper's paradise; you can buy anything from a reproduction icon to designer clothing.

There are three places of cultural interest. The **Museum of Prehistoric Thíra** (https://bit.ly/TheraMuseum; charge) and the **Archaeological Museum** (https://bit.ly/TheraArch; charge) display pottery and other artefacts found on the island. The **Mégaron Gýzi Museum** (+30 22860 23077; charge), north of the cable-car station, is in a beautiful seventeenth-century fortified house. Most exciting of its collections are photographs showing island scenes from before the devastating 1956 earthquake.

Ía

Firá is beautiful, but can get a little oppressive as visitors crowd the narrow streets. A little way northwest is a smaller town where the pace is a little less frantic but be prepared still for crowds. At **Ía** (often written Oia), set on the northern cliffs; many homes are still built into the hillsides, and some have been converted into upmarket art galleries and shops. If you're staying for a sunset drink with great views of the caldera, book ahead.

Pýrgos, Profítis Ilías and Akrotíri

Aside from the stunning views, Santoríni has many more delights, including twelve villages to visit set among agricultural land. The fertile volcanic soil is blanketed by vines producing the renowned local wine, or plants producing tiny, sweet tomatoes. Near the island centre is **Pýrgos** village, with the remains of a Venetian fortress at its core. On a rocky summit to the south stands seventeenth-century **Profítis Ilías Monastery**. The monastery is only opened for morning or evening liturgy, but it is well worth coinciding with the priest to visit. Pride of place goes to a fifteenth-century icon of the prophet Elijah. It also has a museum, which conveys a flavour of monastic life. Unfortunately, the hilltop also bristles with antenna and military paraphernalia, meaning outside photographs are prohibited. On the east coast, **Kamári** and **Périssa** have beaches of fine black or red sand – another legacy of volcanic origins – which heat to a ferocious temperature in summer.

In the far south. near the modern village of Akrotíri, a complete city was discovered dating from before 2000BC (https://odysseus.culture.gr/h/3/eh351.jsp?obj_id=2410; charge). It was totally covered by several feet of ash during the eruption c.1500BC but no human remains have been found, leading scientists to believe that the population managed to escape. Since 1967, it has been painstakingly excavated to reveal a complex and sophisticated society, likely a colony of Minoan Crete.

NOTES

In early 2025, Santorini experienced a series of mild earth tremors that, while causing no lasting damage, led to a dip in tourist numbers. At the time of writing, seismic activity has subsided, and life on the island has returned to normal. This unexpected lull may present a rare opportunity to visit this usually over touristed gem.

Váï Beach is popular with windsurfers

Things to do

Crete is not only an island that offers ancient sites, museums and historic attractions – it also offers a fabulous range of beaches, outdoor activities, shopping and entertainment options. Read on to discover more.

Outdoor activities

Beaches. You'll find hundreds of beaches to suit any visitor on Crete. With everything from tiny coves to lengthy stretches, you can choose to spend your day with swathes of other tourists or have the sand all to yourself at a secluded spot. Beaches in the main resorts have well-organised watersports facilities with jet-skis, water-rides, kayaking and parasailing. The biggest are located around Agios Nikólaos, Liménas Hersónisou, Mália and Réthymno on the north coast. Head east for excellent windsurfing, especially Koureménos near Palékastro.

South-coast resorts tend to be more low-key; beaches are generally smaller, in discrete bays rather than on long stretches of shoreline. You'll find the most diverse range of beach activities at Mátala, a touristy town with an excellent beach, a good sandy bay with waters well regarded by snorkellers, plus fascinating remains of a barely submerged Roman port. On the northern side are high sandstone cliffs where you will find many large Roman tombs cut into the rock. Agía Galíni, Plakiás, Mýrtos and Paleohóra tend to boast a relaxed, laid-back beach atmosphere compared to the more developed northern resorts. These beaches typically feature a mix of sand and pebbles, clear turquoise waters and are often sheltered by surrounding cliffs or hills, offering protection from strong winds, especially compared to the often-windier northern coast and giving a sense of seclusion which attracts independent travellers with fewer large hotels lining the shore.

Sitía is a scenic and unspoiled port on the northeast coast of Crete, about 70km west of Agios Nikólaos, with a beautiful sandy beach, stretching along the town's promenade and gently shelving into calm, shallow waters. It's ideal for families and those seeking a relaxed dip just steps from the cafés and tavernas with a tranquil setting and views of the surrounding hills and fishing boats bobbing offshore.

It's the more remote beaches where you'll find some solitude, usually at the end of steep tracks which may or may not be paved.

Cycling. Mountain biking and cycle touring is becoming increasingly popular. Remember, though, that Crete is extremely mountainous. In some resorts, especially in the west, local companies offer easy cycling tours, with a bus following behind to help you up the hills.

Bike Tours (https://bike-tours.com) offers itineraries such as the "Aegean Discovery: Cycling through Eastern Crete" with a 7 or 14 night option.

Cycle Greece (https://cyclegreece.com) offers a variety of guided and self-guided tours, including options for exploring the coast and mountains.

Book before you go company Exodus Travels (https://

NOTES

Váï, in the far northeastern corner, has beautiful groves of date palms surrounded by a swathe of blonde sand and clear waters, and is a must-see for its stunning beauty. It's a thoroughly secular contrast to the spiritual tranquillity of nearby Toploú monastery, as you lie on the fine sand in the early morning – especially in early spring or late autumn – you could almost imagine yourself on a Caribbean island instead of a Greek one. In summer the beach fills to overflowing, but even then, for a couple of hours at each end of the day you should be able to enjoy Váï the way it should be. Like Elafónisos in the far southwest, famous for its soft, pink sand and a shallow lagoon with undeveloped, pristine stretches perfect for a secluded retreat, Váï gets extremely busy in summer.

exodustravels.com) in the U.K. are known for their cycling holidays through Greece, including Crete, with a specific tour around the East of the island.

Diving and snorkelling. The waters around Crete, especially off the southwest coast, offer interesting diving and snorkelling opportunities for water-lovers with all levels of experience. Although the Mediterranean is overfished and its waters not warm enough to support colourful tropical fish, there are still numerous species to spot in the rocky shallows, including octopus that make their homes in crevices. The remains of many ancient sites lie just off the coast.

The island offers excellent scuba diving

The Greek government is anxious to preserve submerged archeological treasures, so diving is strictly regulated and permitted only with a qualified dive company that oversee underwater activities.

If you have never tried scuba diving before, each dive centre is licensed by the government to offer training in addition to dive supervision for qualified divers. The basic qualification, an Open Water Certificate, normally takes five days to complete. Many centres also offer introductory sessions. Make sure you choose a dive centre affiliated with one of the major certifying bodies: PADI (the Professional Association of Diving Instructors), BSAC (British Sub-Aqua Club) and CMAS (Confédération Mondiale des Activités Subaquatiques) are the most common.

NOTES

Some of the good, reputable dive operators include The Pelagos Dive Centre (https://padi.com/dive-center/crete/pelagos-dive-centre) in Agios Nikólaos, known for its relaxed atmosphere, experienced instructors, and unique "House reef" – the small bay right in front of their dive centre which provides swimming pool conditions and aquarium like marine life, ideal for beginners. They offer all PADI courses up to Divemaster level. There's also Atlantis Diving Centres in Réthymno (https://padi.com/dive-center/greece/diving-center-atlantis) which focus on small group sizes, offering diving and Freediving training with PADI standards for beginners, as well as advanced training with diving trips and Freediving courses.

Walking and hiking

Walking in Crete is amply rewarded with small remote villages, hidden churches and a rural lifestyle to explore. Itineraries can range from short easy walks to steep mountain ascents; however, it's not advisable to head into the high peaks without good maps and a trekking guide. One of the best all-in-one title's is Anavasi Maps' (a shop in central Athens and https://climb-europe.com) *The E4 Cretan Way Walking Guidebook* by Luca Gianotti, with reliable route descriptions and maps.

The European long-distance E4 trail threads the island from Kíssamos to Káto Zákros, and full (or partial) traverses have become increasingly common. Gorge walks are also popular; the Samariá is the busiest and the longest (see page 91). Others include the Imbros and Askífou Gorges near Samariá, the Rouvás Gorge near Záros on Mt Psiloritis, and the Hokhlahiés and Zákros canyons on the east coast. The peninsulas off the northwest coast offer dramatic and interesting walks, for example the trek to Agios Ioánnis chapel on Rodopoú. Akrotíri is not as rugged as Gramvoúsa and Rodopoú, but does have an excellent route between Agía Triáda and Katholikó monasteries. Other rewarding short itineraries can be found around Soúgia (southwest coast).

You'll find local agencies arranging organised hiking tours in many resorts, and plenty of overseas specialist companies offer organised hiking holidays on Crete such as Explore Worldwide (https://explore.co.uk/holidays/walking-in-crete) who offer guided walking holidays including hikes through the Samariá and Záros Gorges, as well as opportunities to experience traditional Cretan hospitality.

Ramble Worldwide (https://rambleworldwide.co.uk/europe/greece/crete/wild-crete) has guided walking holidays focusing on well-loved and off-the-beaten-track paths, with a blend of shorter walks, sightseeing, and quality accommodation on Crete.

Shopping

Shopping is one of the delights of a visit to Crete; souvenirs abound in all quality and price ranges. Most resort souvenir shops cater to mass-market tastes, but you can find locally produced goods, especially along the narrow streets of the old towns, providing hours of browsing. Marked prices can be flexible, particularly in tourist shops and at the beginning and end of the season.

Hiking in the Samaria Gorge

What to buy

Textiles. Crete has a long tradition of handmade textiles. Sheep's wool and goat hair have always been used to produce handwoven material (*yfandá*), clothing and interesting carpets or rugs. The only remaining traditional loom-weaver in Crete is Mihalis Manousakis at his shop *Roka* (Zampelíou 61) in Haniá's Venetian port. If rugged textiles don't appeal, then you'll also find beautiful embroidery such as cotton and linen tablecloths and napkins. The hand-embroidered pieces are the best and most expensive, but this skill is a dying art, so good examples are becoming harder to find.

Dolphins and fish are popular themes, as are stylised images of Greek gods. You'll find particularly interesting ranges in Kritsá and Anógia, and also on the approach to the Dictaean Cave in Lasíthi and in shops in Haniá.

The centuries-old trade of Cretan knife making, Haniá

You'll also have plenty of everyday tablecloths to choose from in markets and the main tourist centres. The Centre of Traditional Folk Art and Culture (Skoufón 20, 28210 92677) in Evraïki, Haniá sells some remarkable modern embroidery.

Leather goods. Crete's cultural traditions include leatherwork, and some families on the island have been making handmade leather goods for generations.

Leather remains extremely good value with bags, purses, luggage and belts found in abundance – try Skrydlóf Street in Haniá to begin comparing quality and prices.

Traditional leather sandals (flat soles with leather straps) are still sold in the streets of Réthymno and Haniá, and are popular because it's more comfortable footwear in summer temperatures than high-tech synthetic materials. There's also a workshop at Kritsá, one of the oldest villages in Crete about 10km inland from Agios Nikólaos, but nowadays modern mass-produced shoes are displacing them. You can also purchase a pair of *stivánia*, Cretan shepherd's boots – almost knee-high, in black leather, with thick soles. They are guaranteed to last decades, and judging by the number of well-worn pairs on feet in the hinterland, that certainly seems true. These are handmade to order, will take about a week to complete, and are accordingly expensive.

NOTES

The Cretan knife is a longstanding cultural symbol, representing both the struggle of the island's people for freedom, and unique craftsmanship. Dating back centuries, Cretan people would go everywhere with a knife in their belt. And while there are no longer any hostile invaders that require locals to brandish these weapons, the tradition endures.

Knives and antiques. Hand-forged Cretan knives are made by various knife-makers, especially in Réthymno and Haniá; stainless-steel blades are fitted to olivewood, bone or horn handles, and are usually inscribed with an appropriate *mantináda* (rhyming couplet). One of the best shops in Haniá's traditional knife-making district (Maherádika) is O Armenis (https://oarmenis.gr/en) at Sifáka 14, owned by Michails Pakhtikos. Making knives since 1912, this shop has been passed down through generations and Michails has been keeping the tradition alive by adding his own character to it as he creates his own unique knives with materials of exceptional quality such as handles made from bones, horns and olive wood.

Cretan history dates back a long time, and if you're lucky, you can find antiquities from the Minoan era – though to be honest, most

NOTES

Greek olive oil is considered among the best in the world, with Crete being a standout, so don't miss the chance to bring home a bottle or two. Ever since Crete was settled several millennia ago, olive oil has been one of the staples of the islanders' diet, and is one reason the Cretan diet is regarded as one of the healthiest in the world. If you're planning on visiting the historic monastery Moní Toploú, you don't need to go elsewhere for olive oil. The gift shop here sells fine oils produced from the monks' own groves.

of what you'll find are copies of museum pieces. That said, there are some wonderful items that come complete with a certificate of authentication, which you may need to show to customs as you depart. To admire more antiques, you can visit museums, and even some hotels and resorts are furnished with rare old pieces. Unique finds from different periods of the island's history, plus vintage furniture and household items, can be discovered in charming shops. For example, Tzangarakis (https://tsangarakis.com/en) at Sifáka 18 in Haniá is Crete's best antique outlet, specialising in watches, jewellery and accessories. Every day, between 3–5pm, they auction off precious estate and contemporary jewellery for reasonable prices. Check out their YouTube channel https://youtube.com/c/GalerieTsangarakisLive to participate with a telephone bid.

Edibles. Olives and olive oil are obvious souvenir choices; the quality of both is considered among the best in Greece. Particularly good are extra virgin cold-pressed oils from Sitía, Toploú and Agía Triáda. Olive oil is more than just something to cook with in Greece – it's a way of life. It has long been a staple, not only of the Greek diet, but the local economy as well. Even urban families have olive groves, gathering their own olives to take to a local mill. Depending on variety and locale, harvesting – either raking off the trees or collecting from black mesh nets that also mark the scenery – occurs between October and

January, with pruning (the wood is a highly prized fuel) soon after.

Cretan cuisine is not just about olives, but also honey and aromatic herbs. Cretans mix honey with thyme, resulting in one of the world's best types of honey. You can find Cretan thyme honey for sale all over the island. One delicious option is to enjoy it in dessert form such as baklavás, an enduring legacy of the Ottomans, consisting of layers of honey-soaked flaky pastry with walnuts. Other herbs that flourish on the island include basil and oregano. Also, dittany (*díktamos*) has been used to make tea on the island for centuries, with other popular bases being sage (*faskomiliá)* and mountain ironwort (*malotíra*).

You will find honey all over the island, but the highest concentration is in the main market areas of major cities like the capital of Iráklio, and there are many local family honey sellers around the island where you'll find a wider variety of honey and some good deals.

Art and icons. Artists flocked to Haniá from the early 1960s onwards, and this has left a legacy in the quality of work on sale here (and to a lesser extent across Crete). There are several galleries displaying work by local and international artists in the Old Town and near the harbour such as the RedD Gallery (https://redd-pr.com) at Anagnostou Mandaka 38, specialising in

Fresh olives are harvested to produce olive oil

Locally grown olives

contemporary art and since 2023, operating their Art Residency Program; inviting select artist to travel to and spend time in Haniá to draw inspiration from the island, or the Mitos Object of Art (https://mitosart.gr/el), housed in a 500 year old Venetian building at Halidon 44, near the harbour, where you can buy handmade bronze and aluminium sculptures, ceramics, blown and fused glass creations, gold and silver jewellery, and reproductions of museum pieces. If you want a primer on modern Greek art, head to the Museum of Contemporary Art of Crete in Réthymno (https://cca.gr; charge). In this old Venetian building you'll find works by various Greek artists, including Lefteris Kanakakis.

A more traditional Greek art form is the icon or religious portrait, usually of a saint or apostle, and lie at the heart of Byzantine or Orthodox worship as they form a focus for prayer. For centuries, icons were popular souvenirs of the European Grand Tour or religious pilgrimage. However, modern production methods using gaudy synthetic colours saw them lose favour. In recent years there has been a rebirth in icon-painting using traditional methods, both for church renovations and for commercial sale. This time-consuming work is exquisite and correspondingly expensive. Orthodoxia (https://orthodoxiashop.gr) at Kriari 19 in central Haniá, a church supply store, is the perfect place to visit to buy anything authentic.

They sell silver icons, silkscreen paintings and traditional icons painted onto wood.

Jewellery. No matter where you travel in the world, artisanal jewellery is often produced specifically for the local culture, and Crete is no different. Here you'll find items designed with an artistry specific to the island's culture and history. For example, Ancient Minoan patterns are common with necklaces, bracelets and rings in matching sets. Both gold and silver are sold by weight, with relatively little extra cost for workmanship. You can also find items featuring precious and semi-precious stones. And best of all, they're available for all budgets.

The House of Amber, (*Kahraman*) at Kondyláki 13, Evraïkí district, Haniá (https://e-kahraman.gr/en) specialises in amber 'worry beads' (*kombológia*). However, you don't need a large budget to buy trinkets; popular street jewellery as sold in the many small shops in the cities sell leather, semi-precious stones and crystals. Alexia Handmade Jewellery at Episkopou Chrysanthou 3, Haniá (https://facebook.com/AlexiaChania) sells unique jewellery such as handmade Byzantine silver, oxidised and gold-plated cubic zirconia rings.

Pottery and ceramics. It's not surprising – given the importance of pottery throughout Crete's history – that it is still a significant industry. Pieces come as small as a ring holder to huge garden pieces. Visit the old town areas of major cities like Iráklio and Réthymno to find the highest concentration of pottery vendors and there are potteries all over the island where you can watch the art of pottery in action. Some places also offer workshop classes, the Spiridi Olive Oil Farm – a family run working rural farm at 2nd km Agios Nikólaos,

NOTES

Crete's art scene merges Greek Orthodox religious imagery with the island's artistic revolution. Haniá boasts several galleries showcasing local art. Most monasteries on Crete create certified copies of their most celebrated icons, and you can also find them in jewellery shops in towns.

Ceramic workshop in the village centre, Margarítes

Elounda 72100, Lassithi, East Crete (https://cretanoliveoilfarm.com/pottery-workshops) is a great place to go and try your hand at making your own gift. They also offer a variety of other workshops worth exploring during your trip such as cheese making, olive pressing, wine tasting and a Cretan Cultural Programme.

In general around the island, both glazed and unglazed cermaics are available; most notable of these is the bright-blue glaze of Haniá ceramics. Traditional designs abound, including marine themes, Minoan designs and Classical Greek imagery. Modern abstract pieces can also be found, particularly in Haniá, where avant-garde potters stock galleries. At Margarítes village you can watch the potters at work and buy from their workshops.

Olive-wood items. Crete's abundant olive trees not only produce high-quality oil, but also durable wood, used to create hand-crafted utensils and souvenirs. Annual prunings and heftier trunk wood are fashioned into a myriad of useful or decorative items: cutting boards, cooking utensils, napkin rings, candle holders. Cutting boards should ideally be one piece and not made of glued-together sections. Large pieces require long seasoning and are hard to work, so they don't come cheaply. Art on Olive Wood (October 28, Agios Nikólaos; 28410 25168) sells many objects d'art and practical olive wood items. If you head to Iráklio's Old Town, you can browse countless boutiques, bazaars and street stalls selling all manner of olive-wood items. Serving bowls and cutlery are particularly good value for money, and high quality.

Children's Crete

Aside from museums, ancient sites, churches and beach visits, there's also lots of fun to be had for younger members of the family. Greek society is very family-oriented, and children will be very welcome at tavernas and cafés, irrespective of the time of day or night.

Beach activities are well-organised and abundant along the northern coast, offering all types of watersports and rides. The best sandy beaches are at the resort town of Mália, Réthymno, Georgioúpoli and Váï. South-coast resorts such as Plakiás, Paleohóra and Mátala have good beaches and plenty of snorkelling opportunities for older children.

Children (and young adults at heart) will enjoy the waterparks near Haniá (Limnoupolis; https://limnoupolis.gr), Iráklio (https://watercity.gr) and Liménas Hersonísou (https://acquaplus.gr), designed to keep them occupied for hours. Best to book tickets in advance on their sites.

Trips along the coast in colourful *caïques* offer the chance to enjoy a cooling breeze and an alternative view of the island. Castles such as the Koúles in Iráklio, Réthymno's Fortezza and Frangokástello allow imaginations to run wild.

The rural lifestyle of the interior – watching goats filing past,

Enjoying family time on the beach

or donkeys working hard for their owners – will delight urban children. Plus, there's no entry fee for this type of experience, a mere appreciation of tradition. Older children may enjoy gorge walks Many larger hotels have children's clubs and crêches for toddlers, too.

Culture

Entertainment. Numerous fairs and festivals take place throughout the year. Local tourist offices will have details of what's happening during your stay on Crete. Each community celebrates its patron saint's day, when the saint's icon is usually paraded through the streets. After a solemn religious service, the rest of the day (or evening) is given over to revelry. These are the best places to see traditional Cretan dances and live music, and to join in with local people having fun.

Music and dance. For many, Greek music and dance is inexorably linked to the film *Zorba the Greek*, with Anthony Quinn performing the *syrtáki*, an amalgam of several traditional dances, accompanied by the *bouzoúki*. Taverna owners' habit of playing this tune at high volume does a great disservice to the rich and venerable music tradition of Crete, where traditional instrumentalists and singers are held in high regard.

Musical rhythms throughout Greece are very different from the 'four beats to a bar' that characterises western music, and can be difficult for foreign would-be dancers to follow. Song lyrics, usually sung by men, refer not only to the hard life of shepherds, farmers and fishermen, but also touch on love (especially unrequited) – an element of sentimentality rarely expressed directly at other times.

Crete's main traditional musical instrument is the *lýra*, a three-stringed lap fiddle, played upright. It is usually accompanied by the *laoúto*, a long-necked, fretted development of the Arab *oud* (lute), and sometimes the *askomandoúra* (bagpipes with two chanters but no drone). These instruments typically accompany *mantinádes*, sung rhyming couplets. Some of these have been passed down through generations of Cretans, but many are improvised on the spot. The men of the western Lefká Óri range sing sparsely accompanied songs, the *rizítika*, elegies for battles and heroic personages. The mountain men also have their distinctive, martial *pendozális* dance; in Réthymno and other coastal towns, the pan-Aegean *soústa* is common.

Chanting epic poetry is also a long-standing Cretan tradition. The seventeenth-century epic *Erotokritos*, written by Vitsentzos Kornaros

ZORBA'S DANCE

The film *Zorba the Greek* brought international fame to author Nikos Kazantzakis' 1946 novel. Michael Cacoyannis, a Greek film-maker of Cypriot origin, made the film in 1964 with Anthony Quinn in the leading role as Alexis Zorba. His famous *syrtáki* dance scene dismayed the islanders, as it's not a genuine Cretan dance. The indigenous *pendozáli* proved too difficult for the American actor to learn, so soundtrack composer Mikis Theodorakis came up with a simple but danceable melody in its place. The hordes of tourists who later came to Crete asked to see a dance that did not actually exist, but hoteliers and the music industry moved quickly to oblige them. *Syrtáki* is performed at today's 'Cretan evenings', and recordings of the catchy tune are available everywhere. But be aware it's not the traditional dance of Crete at all.

in local dialect, is the most popular of these, having inspired many modern Greek poets, and has been set to music repeatedly.

Nightlife. Good places to see traditional music include the midsummer festivals of the largest towns (see page 113). Larger hotels stage weekly 'Greek nights', or run excursions to events at village tavernas. The music and dance is usually of a high standard, although surroundings are hardly authentic. More atmospheric is *Tavern To Adespoto* in Haniá at the corner of Sifáka and Melchisedek, which offers live music every evening from 7.30pm (https://adespotochania.gr). An intimate venue for all kinds of acoustic music is the first-floor bar of the *Pagopoieio*, which also offers executive suites, on Platía Agíou Títou in central Iráklio (https://pagopoieion.gr).

A tradition of dance

In far eastern Crete, near Palékastro, another unlikely but wonderful acoustic stage is Maridatis (https://maridatis.gr), a musical taverna behind the eponymous cove, featuring Greek performers every Friday and Saturday in summer.

For real traditional music enthusiasts, there's an excellent musical workshop centre in Houdétsi village, near Iráklio; see https://labyrinthmusic.gr. More casually, patronize the excellent Aerakis CD shop at Platia Korai 14 in Iráklio (https://aerakis.net), which specialises in local musicians.

Festivals and events

Each Cretan community celebrates its own saint's day (often more than one), there are too many such celebrations, called *panigýria*, to list here. Below are the major events occurring across the island.

6 January: *Theofánia* (Epiphany). Youths dive for a crucifix thrown into harbours.

February/March: Street carnivals with floats and masquers in Réthymno and Iráklio on the two weekends before Lent.

March/May: Easter. *Epitáfios* processions on Good Friday; effigy of Judas burned on Saturday; in churches the sacred flame passes to worshippers' candles Saturday midnight; on Sunday a lamb is barbecued.

23 April: Ágios Geórgios (St George), patron saint of shepherds; sheep-shearing festival in Así Goniá.

20–27 May: Battle of Crete commemorated at Máleme and Haniá.

23–24 June: St John the Baptist/Midsummer's Eve, celebrated with bonfires which are leapt over.

Late June: Casa dei Mezzo Music Festival (https://casadeimezzo.com). Classical chamber concert series.

July: Renaissance Festival of dramatic and musical performances at Réthymno.

July–August: Kornaria Cultural Festival in Sitía.

July–September: Iráklio festival, with theatrical and music events.

15 August: *Kímisi tís Panagías* (Dormition of the Virgin). Celebrated throughout Crete, at churches dedicated to the Virgin.

25 August: Ágios Títos (St Titus, patron saint of Crete). Procession in Iráklio.

29 August: Ágios Ioánnis (John the Baptist). Pilgrimage on foot (4-hr round trip) to Ágios Ioánnis chapel on the Rodopoú Peninsula.

28 October: *Óhi* Day. Celebrates Greek defiance of Italians in World War II.

7–9 November: Commemoration of the Arkádi Monastery explosion with a fireworks display.

Food and drink

Since Crete was settled several millennia ago, its people have relied on staples such as olive oil, fragrant herbs, wild greens, seafood, lamb or goat meat, and an abundance of fresh garden vegetables, fruit, pulses and nuts. Combine these with more recent Venetian and Ottoman influences, and you have an interesting cuisine. The island shares many recipes with the Greek mainland, but it also has numerous ingredients and dishes found nowhere else.

Today, the traditional Cretan diet is considered to be one of the healthiest in the world, and it is well worth following locals to the better eateries to try it. Cretan gastronomy offers a vibrant culinary scene rooted in centuries-old traditions and an unwavering commitment to local produce. Whether you're tucking into slow-cooked lamb in a mountain taverna or sipping a chilled glass of *rakí* by the sea, food here is a celebration of the land and its people. Since 2021, a wave of exciting new openings has added a contemporary flair to the island's gastronomic landscape. Think farm-to-table eateries in Haniá's old town, natural wine bars in Iráklio, and innovative tasting menus highlighting ancient Minoan ingredients with a modern twist. Across the island, younger chefs and restaurateurs are returning to their roots, blending

NOTES

If you have to go English, tavernas in resort areas may offer a full English breakfast as well as lunch and dinner or Sunday roast. Typically, Greeks don't eat breakfast – a coffee and *friganiés* (melba toast) or a baked pastry is about as much as they'll indulge in. Lunch is eaten between 2.30 and 4pm, followed by a siesta before work begins again at 5.30pm. Dinner is eaten late, usually from 9.30pm onwards, and some establishments take last orders as late as midnight. You'll find most tavernas are closed on Sunday evenings and part or all of Monday.

bold creativity with authentic Cretan flavours, making this an ideal time to discover what's cooking on Crete.

Top ten things to try

1. Olive oil

Dried thyme and oregano for tea

Olive oil has long been a staple not only of the Greek diet, but also the local economy, and this is particularly true on the islands. Even urban families have olive groves, gathering their own olives to take to a local mill. Depending on variety and locale, harvesting – either raking off the trees or collecting from black mesh nets that also mark the scenery – occurs between October and January, with pruning (the wood is a highly prized fuel) soon after. Head to a local monastery to buy reproductions of olive oils the monks produced from their own groves centuries ago.

2. Mountain tea

Greek mountain tea has a unique flavour that is both earthy and slightly floral, and is enjoyed for its soothing and calming properties. *Malotira* is made from the dried flowers, leaves and stems of the Sideritis plant, which is native to the Cretan mountains. It is known for its numerous health benefits, including its antioxidant properties and its potential to aid digestion and boost the immune system. When you drink a freshly brewed tea or coffee in Crete, don't drink right to the bottom as that's where the leaves/grounds settle. Instead, enjoy drinking it slowly and savouring it. You can purchase tea from any supermarket rather than pay to have it in a café and still have some left to bring home.

3. Snails

Snails (*hokhlí*) from Crete are much prized throughout Greece, and can reputedly be prepared in no less than forty different ways. They're eaten fresh only during the warmer months when they're dormant, or immediately after rain when they emerge, but also served from frozen at Lent. Methods of cooking include scalded in salted water; stewed with potatoes and courgettes; fried in rosemary, garlic and oil; or best of all, cooked with tomatoes, potatoes and thyme in a dish called *egíni*.

Snails are a local delicacy

One of the most traditional snail dishes on Crete is *hochlioi bourbouristi* (burbling snails). This involves frying the snails and finishing them with vinegar. They can also be cooked in red wine and garlic. Plenty of restaurants in Iráklio Old Town serve snails, and you can head just outside the city to Snail Farm and Fun (https://snailfarmandfun.com) – not a particular tourist destination, more a small working farm run by a couple and where you can pick fresh snails to cook at home.

4. Meze (mezédhes)

For a true taste of Greece, tuck into a *mezé* platter of starters and dips accompanied by a glass of *ouzo* or *tsípouro*. The most common appetisers on Crete are *tzatzíki* – a yoghurt dip flavoured with garlic, cucumber and mint; *dolmádes*, vine leaves stuffed with rice and vegetables – and sometimes mince – which can be served hot (with *avgolémono* sauce, made from eggs and lemon) or cold (with yoghurt); *taramosaláta*, cod-roe paste blended with breadcrumbs, olive oil and lemon juice; *yígandes*, large beans in tomato sauce; *keftedákia*, small meatballs flavoured with spices; *kalamarákia*, deep-fried squid; and *plevrótous*, oyster mushrooms.

NOTES

Pick up snails at the market and try cooking them on your own. All you need to do is to soak them in cold water for an hour, then place them in a saucepan and cook with the other ingredients.

Some of the best and cheapest mezé, or *orektiká*, are frequently meat-free: *fáva* is yellow split peas puréed, served with chopped onions, lemon wedges and olive oil, while *mavromátika* (black-eyed peas) are boiled and then served chilled.

5. Fish and seafood

Seafood can be one of the highlights of Greece, with a variety of locally caught fish, such as red mullet, bream, or grouper, as well as squid and octopus. You'll find the highest concentration of fine seafood restaurants in the major cities of Crete, like Iráklio and Réthymno.

When ordering fish and seafood, there are some tips to bear in mind. The standard procedure is to go to the glass cooler and pick your specimen, then have it weighed (uncleaned) in your presence. Overcharging, especially where a printed menu is absent, is not uncommon, so have weight and price confirmed clearly. Taverna owners often comply only minimally with the requirement to

A selection of appetising meze

indicate when seafood is frozen – look for the abbreviation "kat", "k" or just an asterisk on the Greek-language side of the menu. If the price, almost invariably quoted by the kilo, seems too good to be true, it's almost certainly farmed.

6. Grilled meat

Cretans have long relied on food from the land such as lamb, rabbit and goat. Barbecued dishes include whole chicken, *loukánika* (sausages, the best are from the Sfakiá district in Haniá), and sides of lamb or *soúvla* (rotisserie-cooked pork), all done to perfection. *Brizóla* – pork or veal – is a basic cutlet; lamb or goat chops, however, are called *païdákia*.

Roasted or barbecued lamb is the traditional post-Easter fare. Stewed goat (*yídha vrastí*) is also a very popular village dish, often served with a side of *gamopílafo* (sticky white rice). Meat stews include *kléftiko* (braised lamb with tomatoes), *stifádo* (braised beef with onions) and *giouvétsi* (meat baked with lozenge-shaped *kritharáki* pasta). Each comes in a small clay pot that keeps the contents piping hot.

7. Cretan cheeses

Most Cretan cheeses are made from cow's, ewe's or goat's milk, or often blends of two kinds. The best-known cheese is *féta*, featured in every Greek salad or served alone garnished with olive oil and oregano. *Graviéra* and *kefalotýri* are the most common, hard grating cheeses, varying in sharpness. There are also many sweet soft kinds of cheese such as *manoúri* and *anthótyro*. Served at many tavernas is *stáka* – a clotted cream made from goat's milk, and *tyrokafterí*, a spicy cheese dip. Rather than buy from artisanal specialist shops, supermarket varieties are just as good and will give you a good introduction to local cheeses.

8. Sweet treats

Cretan desserts can be prepared sweet or savoury, and use ingredients also used in traditional savoury dishes such as olive oil, nuts, fruits and honey. At local tavernas, satisfy your sweet tooth with honey, fresh fruit and cream.

9. Fresh produce

Cretans love showcasing their seasonal produce, with few imported fruits, and plenty of local fresh vegetables and wild herbs.

NOTES

Quick, meat-based snacks include *gýros* (thin slices of meat cut from a vertical skewer and served with garnish and *tzatzíki* in pitta bread), or *souvláki* (small chunks of meat cooked on a skewer). These delicious and simple Cretan and Greek staples could be considered the Greek fast-food equivalent of McDonalds.

NOTES

A *zaharoplastío* (a cross between café and patisserie) dishes out some decadent sweets – one of the more enduring legacies of the Ottomans: *baklavás*, layers of honey-soaked flaky pastry with walnuts; *kataïfi*, 'shredded wheat' filled with chopped almonds and honey; *galaktoboúreko*, custard pie; *ravaní*, honey-soaked sponge cake; or *loukoumádhes*, deep-fried batter puffs dusted with cinnamon and dipped in syrup. The better ones usually offer an amazing variety of pastries or cream-and-chocolate confections with coffee and a limited range of alcohol.

Wild greens like *stífnos*, *stamnagáthi* (spiny chicory, often paired with meat) and *askolýmbri* (golden thistle) are especially popular. Fruit platters after meals typically feature watermelon or Persian melon in summer; grapes or pears in autumn; sliced apples with cinnamon much of the year; and citrus or maybe even some strawberries in early spring. It's a joy to wander through the main agoras in the towns to see the fresh produce on sale. Similar to an Italian bruschetta, *dakos* is a refreshing and delicious Cretan appetizer of a round of hard bread with fresh tomatoes literally squeezed onto it, topped with feta cheese, olive oil and oregano.

10. Cretan wine, beer and spirits, and non-alcoholic drinks

Greek wine-making dates back over three thousand years and has improved significantly in recent decades. Many wineries produce under twenty thousand bottles per year. Cretan wine, in particular, was celebrated throughout antiquity, only losing favour in relatively modern times. Red, white or rosé are offered in full, half or quarter-litre measures, either in colourful aluminium vessels (*katroútza*) or in glass flagons. Quality varies considerably across the island.

As for spirits, Cretans favour their own, *rakí*. It's distilled like ouzo from grape pressings, but is unflavoured, but may have a touch of anise, cinnamon, pear essence or fennel and is the least expensive tipple on the island, often cheaper than bottled water. Many tavernas offer a small *karafáki* (tumbler) of it on the house at the conclusion of the meal whereas ouzo – always flavoured with anise, is always taken as an aperitif with ice and water. A compound in its anise flavouring makes the mix turn harmlessly cloudy. The alcohol strength of either spirit ranges from 40–50 percent.

Hot coffee is served *ellínikós* or 'Greek' style, served in small cups. It will automatically arrive *glykós* (sweet) unless you order *métrios* (medium) or *skétos* (without sugar). Don't drink right to the bottom as that's where the grounds settle. Instant coffee *(nes)* has made big inroads in Greece; more appetising is *frappé*, cold instant coffee, whipped up in a blender with evaporated milk, rather like a coffee milkshake.

Juices are usually from cartons rather than freshly squeezed. One of the most refreshing drinks is Cretan mineral water, fresh from mountain springs.

A local favourite: rakí

Where to eat

Crete has a range of eateries specialising in certain types of food and drink. Although the boundaries between them are blurring, the following explains what you can expect to find.

Fresh dishes to share

A *psistaría* offers charcoal-grilled meat dishes, plus a limited selection of salads and meze (*mezédes*). The *tavérna* is a more elaborate eatery, often family run, and inviting longer sit-down meals of pre-cooked, steam-tray dishes known as *mageireftá*, as well as a few grills and bulk wine. A *psárotaverna* specialises in fish and seafood.

An *ouzerí* purveys not just that quintessentially Greek alcoholic drink, but also the meze dishes that complement it – locals are well aware that *oúzo* should not be drunk on an empty stomach. Octopus, olives, a piece of cheese or a platter of small fried fish are traditional accompaniments but you will find other variations. A *mezedopolío* is a more elaborate *ouzerí* where food takes precedence.

All restaurants render a cover charge. This includes a serving of bread and is usually no more than €1 per person – if you can, try *paximádia* (the traditional Cretan dry bread) or *dákos* (barley rusks), the latter often the basis of a popular salad (called *koukouvágia* in Réthymno district).

The *kafeníon* is the Greek coffee shop, traditionally a men-only domain, and still the case in the inland villages. Usually very plainly decorated with old wooden tables with no tablecloths and chairs, they are often the venues for political debate and serious backgammon games.

To help you order

Could we have a table? **Boroúme na éhoume éna trapézi?**
Could we order, please? **Na parangiloúme, parakaló?**
a half litre **misó kilo**
I'm a vegetarian **Íme hortofágos**
Bon appetite **Kalí órexi**
Cheers! **Giámas!**
The bill, please **To logariazmó, parakaló**

Menu reader

arní lamb
avgá eggs
barboúni red mullet
boútero butter
býra beer
domátes tomatoes
eliés olives
fasolákia runner beans
froúta fruit
gala milk
garídes small shrimp
gemistá stuffed
hirinó pork
hórta boiled greens
katsíki goat
kotópoulo chicken
kounélli rabbit
krasí wine
kréas meat
lahaniká vegetables
melitzánes aubergines
moskhári beef
oktapódi octopus
orektiká starters
pagotó ice cream
(pagoméno) neró (chilled) water
piperiés peppers
psári fish
psitó roasted
psomí bread
revýthia chickpeas
rýzi rice
saláta salad
sídi vinegar
soúpa soup
spanáki spinach
sta kárvouna grilled
sto foúrno baked
thalassiná seafood
tiganitó fried
tyrí cheese
tyrópittes cheese pies
xifías swordfish
xýgalo stuffed cabbage leaves
záhari sugar

Places to eat

The following price ranges reflect the average cost of a two-course meal (per person) and a beer or share of bottled wine or *raki*. Except where indicated, reservations are rarely necessary (or even possible) – one waits, or an extra table may be fitted in. Unless indicated otherwise, all establishments accept card payment.

€€€€ = over 45 euros
€€€ = 35–45 euros
€€ = 22–35 euros
€ = under 22 euros

Iráklio and central Crete

Alekos Behind Agía Pelagía church, Vóri, 28920 91094. After visiting Phaistos and Agía Triáda, head for this secluded village taverna for a historic taste of Crete. The setting – a courtyard with tables and cushioned bench seating, and interior with a fireplace – is matched by the food: hearty portions of deftly executed recipes. A wood-burning oven bakes goat or kid dishes (ordered in advance). Open daily for both lunch and dinner. Cash only. **€€**

Giakoumis Fotíou Theodosáki 5-8, Iráklio, https://facebook.com/giakoumis Estiatorio. Popular classic market taverna specialising in succulent lamb chops, crispy potatoes, seasonal salads and equally good rosé or white bulk wine. Cash only. **€**

Ippokambos Sofoklí Venizélou 3, Iráklio, https://ippokamposseafood.gr. Highly regarded *ouzerí* fantastically situated by the Venetian harbour. Excellent meze (including snails), reasonably priced fish and seafood, plus a winning service. Understandably, it gets busy, so go early to avoid disappointment as it doesn't take reservations. April–Nov Tues–Sun lunch and dinner. **€€**

Kirkor Lion (Morosíni) Fountain Square, Iráklio, 28102 42705. Armenian-run stall with outdoor tables opposite the fountain, serving succulent *bougátsa* (custard pastry), *tyrópittes* (cheese pies) and good coffees since 1922. Daily from dawn until evening. **€**

Pagopoieio Papagiamali 1, Platía Agíou Títou, Iráklio, https://pagopoieion.gr. Meaning 'ice factory', this intimate venue for acoustic music also serves delicious authentic fair such as burrata salad, creamy mushroom risotto, beef tartare, and tender fillet. **€€€**

Peskesi Kapetan Charalampi 6-8, Iráklio, https://peskesicrete.gr/el. Set in a beautifully restored stone mansion along a quiet, cobbled pedestrian street in the heart of *Iráklio*, Peskesi offers authentic Cretan farm to table cuisine from their own farm near Gouves. Don't miss the yogurt-braised lamb, a favourite with patrons due to the tender meat and traditional recipe. **€€**

Taverna Istorikón Kapetanaki Georgiou, Archanes, 2810 751 115. Great for a lunch stop in this tiny traditional village. Expect tapas (meze) style such as dolmades, Cretan sausage, stuffed peppers and the ubiquitous meatballs. **€**

Vegera Zaros village, Iráklio, https://vegerazaros.gr/index.php/en/restaurant. A renowned vegetarian restaurant with some meat options. The meal unfolds like this: your party gets a pitcher of cool water, then come salads, a plate of assorted cheeses and olives, several home-cooked local dishes, and finally: pastries and *raki*. All ingredients are organic and mostly seasonal. Definitely worth a visit. **€**

Votomos Near Lake Vótomos, Záros, 69748 67233. Trout specialists, relying on their own fish farm, though there are also lamb and chicken dishes. The setting, in the Psiloritis foothills, is idyllic, and as such it's a popular spot. April–Oct daily for lunch and dinner, winter weekends only. **€€**

Ágios Nikólaos and the east

Angistri Angathiás village centre, near Palékastro, 69736 04499. Some of the cheapest and freshest fish in the region, straight from the owner's boat. His son and daughter grill and serve respectively. A few good grilled meat dishes available as well, plus superb views from the terrace by day. **€€**

Blue Café On the rocks past the western end of the beach, Léndas, Tel. 6972 822 152. A romantic spot to lounge over evening drinks while watching the moon rise over the bay, as people have been doing here since the resort's earliest days. Limited menu. **€€**

Gioma Meze Dionisou Solomou 12, Ágios Nikólaos, https://giomameze.com. Delightful fish and meze restaurant overlooking the harbour. Try their mushroom stew as an appetiser, shrimp tartare with creamed avocado or braised lamb shank. **€€**

Káto Zákros Bay Waterfront, Káto Zákros, https://facebook.com/p/Kato-Zakros-Bay-Taverna-Nikos-Platanakis. Tellingly, this taverna at one of eastern Crete's remotest bays gets the most local clientele forits home-grown vegetables and poultry, fair prices and decent quality. The place to be to see local life in action. April–Oct, open all day. Cash only. **€€**

Ta Kohylia East quay, Mókhlos, 28430 94432. A reliable choice amongst several establishments here, also the oldest (founded 1902). Expect fresh artichokes in spring, stews, and daily casseroles like stuffed vegetables or *mousakás*. Feb–Nov, lunch and dinner. **€€**

Levante Stratigoú Samaíl 38, Ierápetra, https://levante-taverna.gr. The most reliable of the string of tavernas behind the seafront. Castle views are matched by homely dishes like milk-based *xýgalo*, stuffed cabbage leaves, *papoutsáki* and *omathiés* (rice-and-offal sausage). **€€**

Taverna El Greco On the beach, Léndas, www.lentas-elgreco.com. A particularly good restaurant with a large leafy terrace above the beach. The food is mostly traditional Greek – the day's baked dishes are on display in the kitchen – but cooked with exceptional care using the best local ingredients. There's anunusually good wine list, too, and they also have rooms. **€€**

Zygos Kaló Horió centre, near Istron, 28410 61389. Whole goats roasting on spits out front announce this traditional taverna, with the management sourcing ingredients from their own farm. It can get raucous in high season, but Dimítris is a great host. **€€**

Réthymno, Haniá, the southwest

Ambrosia Lake Kourná, https://ambrosialakekournas.com. Forego sea views in favour of panoramic views of *Lake Kourná*. Amphitheatrically staged along the shores of the lake, it's a favourite to while away the day. Breakfasts and fresh juices through to lunch and dinners of seafood and fresh fish to home-made pizza and grilled meat dishes made with ingredients from local producers. The spaghetti with lobster and grilled salmon are a favourite. **€-€€**

Breeze Kissamos waterfront, https://breezecafe.gr. Great waterfront spot along this popular beach stretch serving breakfasts such as fruit and granoula bowls, waffles to omelettes, and coffees from early AM then brunches and evening dinners with chicken dishes, burgers, pastas and risottos. It's the view and rooftop bar for cocktails that make this the pull. **€-€€**

Café Galero Rimondi Fountain, Réthymno, https://facebook.com/CafeGalero. Operating since 1926 and although very touristy and prices for simple foods such as burgers and a coffee reflecting this, it's a popular spot to take a break and people watch at the Rimondi Fountain in Réthymno. **€-€€**

Ta Chalkina Aktí Tombazi 29–30, old harbour, Haniá, https://chalkina.com. Tucked between the tourist traps of the two Venetian ports is this *rakádiko*, well attended for titbits like eggplant roulade, *marathópita* (fennel pie) and *apáki*. Oddly, their bulk wine is preferable to their *raki*. Daily noon–1am. Cash only. **€€**

Dounias Main access road, Drakona, https://ntounias.gr. A picturesque family-owned small restaurant off the beaten track at the foot of the White Mountains. The Dounias family runs their own farm, produces olive oil and uses only local ingredients in their traditional, rustic dishes. Slow food and slow service, but a unique dining experience overall. **€€**

Eleasthea Voukolies, 2 km to Paleochora, Haniá, https://eleasthea.gr. The restaurant is a 9-min drive from the nearby village of Vouves, famous for the island's oldest olive tree. Family run, its terrace seating looks out over the swathes of olive groves and is a fantastic place to dine on fresh bread, traditional Cretan carbonara and snails. Their menu is extensive and has a vegetarian option too including many salad choices. **€€**

Ntourountous Bakery & Coffee Shop Chatzimichali Giannari 41, Haniá, https://ntourountous.gr. This local favourite coffee shop, their debut family bakery in the village of Sfakia, sells a good selection of coffees, cakes and homemade *kalitsounia* (sweet or savoury Cretan small cheese or herb pastries, a popular and beloved staple traditionally made with mizithra cheese, herbs, or honey). **€**

Oinoa Wine Restaurant Theotokopoulou 63, Haniá, https://facebook.com/oinoa.gr. Daily 8am–2am. Perfect for a romantic dinner or special night out. Oinoa's menu focuses on Cretan and Mediterranean cuisine with a modern twist–try slow-cooked lamb or fresh seafood paired with a glass from the expertly curated Greek wine list. Feel at home in their cosy stone interior and come for a refined dining experience in the heart of Old Town Haniá. **€€€€**

Prima Plora Akrotiriou 4, Réthymno, https://primaplora.gr/en. This organic restaurant sources ingredients from local, small-scale producers and its location by Réthymno Harbour, overlooking the Fortress makes it a great dinner spot. Try their seafood linguine or a whole selection of sushi dishes. **€€€**

Raki ba Raki Arampatzóglou 17, Réthymno, https://facebook.com/1600RakiBaRaki. A great spot in the heart of Réthymno Old Town with traditional 1950s style Greek taverna décor, serving delights such as fava, grilled octopus and vegetarian dishes like stuffed aubergine. Ask for dishes of the day. **€€**

Red Jane Bakery Kidonias 101, Haniá, https://instagram.com/redjaneproject. An artisanal bakery opened in a repurposed interwar factory in downtown Haniá has coffees, pasteries and sourdough delights to die for. Loved by visitors and locals alike. **€**

Rembetiko Taverna Sougia seafront, https://rembetiko-taverna-business.site. At this lovely taverna on the seafront of Sougia, you can dine in the sheltered courtyard on traditional Cretan staples such as lamb shank, rabbit or *dolmádes*. **€€**

Strata Portou 54, Haniá, 28210 93830. A popular tavern in Hania's Venetian harbour, usually packed as the food is really good. Huge portions, salads are conspicuously big, so don't order too much. Excellent service and friendly atmosphere. Occasional concerts add to the atmosphere in the evening. **€€**

Tamam Zambeliou 49, Evraïkí district, Haniá, https://tamamrestaurant.com. This former *hamam* built in 1645 contains one of the best, most atmospheric restaurants in town. The fare is Cretan, with Mediterranean/Middle Eastern specialities like Iranian pilaf, plus oodles of choice for vegetarians. **€€€€**

Taverna Kalomirakis Part of Elafonissi Resort, Kandanos Selinos, Elafonissi, https://elafonisi-resort.com/restaurant. Part of the Elafonissi resort, this family run taverna is open to non-guests for breakfast, lunch and dinner offering a selection of meat, fish, pasta, salads and vegetarian dishes such as Imam (aubergine stuffed with cheese) and pork or chicken souvlaki. **€-€€**

Tavern To Adespoto Corner of Sifáka and Melchisedek, Haniá, https://adespotochania.gr. Open-air restaurant and music taverna located amongst the leafy ruins of a historic Venetian townhouse in Haniá's Old Town. Great views of the City Walls and steps away from the Venetian Harbour. Try their snails with rosemary and Cretan vinegar, and their local draft beer such as Charma Larger from the Cretan Brewery. **€-€€**

The Third Eye 50m inland from west beach, south end, Paleohóra, https://thirdeye-paleochora.com. A remarkable vegetarian restaurant with an extensive and imaginative Asian/Indian menu plus a range of desserts. Breakfast also avaioable for early visitors. Occasional concerts by night. Cash only. **€€**

To Maridaki Daskalogianni 33, Haniá, https://tomaridaki.gr/en. A very popular seafood taverna, thanks to the fact they only prepare what's at the seafood market daily, for example fresh cuttlefish, cod, clams and shrimps. All served with a wide variety of vegetables, and their salads are popular too. Meat dishes also available. **€**

Zorbas Behind the giant eucalyptus, near bus stop, Stavrós, Akrotíri peninsula, 2821 039402. Generally, you should run a mile from tavernas so-named, but this one's the real deal – the most locally attended of several on this sandy cove, where the disastrous log-transport scene of *Zorba the Greek* was filmed. There's a good range of seafood, cheeses, lamb dishes and hearty vegetable casseroles in big portions. Open all year round. Cash only. **€**

Travel essentials

Practical information

Accessible Travel

Beaches & Water Access Greece, including Crete, has made encouraging strides in sea access for visitors with mobility challenges. Several popular beaches, Agii Apostoli (near Haniá), Rethymno, Ammoudara (Iráklio region) and Kokkino Pyrgos, are equipped with **SEATRAC** systems (https://seatrac.gr/en/beach-directory). This assistive technology enables independent entry into the water via a beach-side seat and track, meaning users can enjoy a swim safely, without assistance. SEATRAC effectively levels the shoreline, promoting inclusivity for all ages and abilities. They're part of wider efforts to make Crete's coastal scenery fully accessible.

Beyond SEATRAC, beaches like Elafonisi also offer accessible features through tour operators such as Eria Travel (https://eria-travel.gr) who provide floating wheelchairs (*tirallo*), accessible changing rooms, and lifeguard-supervised assistance.

Planning & Travel Support It's worth noting that "accessible" in Greece often depends on local conditions. For example, Haniá's old town is cobbled, yet its harbour is paved so some parts are more accessible than others.

Consider using some of the below agences before you travel to help you in planning and get support before you go. Another goof resource is Limitless Travel (https://limitlesstravel.org) who organise inclusive programmes on Crete with accessible hotels, transport, specialist equipment, and round-the-clock support ensuring a worry-free and fulfilling holiday.

Tours & Excursions Specialist travel agencies operating in Crete such as **Disabled Accessible Travel** (https://disabledaccessibletravel.com), **Eria Travel** (https://eria-travel.gr), and **Accessible Travel Greece** (https://accessibletravel.gr) provide a wide range of wheelchair-friendly excursions. These include guided visits to Haniá's Venetian harbor, Rethymno's Fortezza, Iráklio 's archaeological sites and aquarium, or accessible trips to natural wonders like the White Mountains and Elafonisi beach

Tailored tours often include adapted transport, private driver-guides with Wi-Fi, and accessible entry to cultural landmarks. Walkers seeking flat, paved promenades in places like Rethymno can enjoy leisurely sightseeing without obstacles

Accommodation

Hotels: Many resort hotels have contracts with tour operators. If travelling between mid-July and early September, always make a firm reservation before arrival to avoid disappointment. October prices are generally much lower than at peak season. Most resort hotels close from November to March inclusive, although some hotels in the larger northern coastal towns stay open all year. Hotel booking websites can yield significant discounts at any time such as https://booking.com.

Rooms, apartments and studios: Except at the top end of the quality scale, the vast majority of accommodation in Crete is in modern, purpose-built blocks of rooms, studios or apartments, usually family-owned and run, simply furnished, yet almost always immaculately clean. The fancier places may be small complexes built around a pool and a small bar or restaurant. Apartments and studios will have some form of cooking facilities, larger apartments may have up to three bedrooms, making them ideal for families.

In the UK, some of the best agencies specialising in packages for high-quality self-catering premises, both villas and hotels include Pure Crete (https://purecrete.com), Sunvil (https://sunvil.co.uk), The Villa Collection (https://gicthevillacollection.com) and Cachet Travel (https://cachet-travel.co.uk).

I'd like a single/double room with bath/shower **Tha íthela éna monóklino/díklino me bánio/dous**
How much (does it cost)? **Póso káni?**

Airports

International, charter and domestic flights to Crete serve the airports at **Iráklio** (Heraklion; HER), for central and eastern resorts, and **Haniá** (CHQ) for the western part of the island. The airport at **Sitía** (JSH), in the far east, only has domestic flights as the airport is not equipped to handle international aircraft. The only option to reach town is a taxi, unless you want to brave the 1.2km (0.7-miles) downhill walk into town.

Iráklio International Airport (aka Iráklio or "Nikos Kazantzakis" (https://Iráklio-airport.gr/en) is the biggest of all three, and can get very crowded, especially in peak season. There's a bus servicing the 5km (3 miles) route to and from Iráklio KTEL central bus stop in the centre of town until late at night (https://heraklion-airport.info/bus), but the bus station from the airport is located a small walk just outside the airport grounds on the central road, so it's not the most convenient but is the cheapest option.

There is also a bus from Haniá airport (https://chq-airport.gr/en/category-detailed/ctg_id-69/nd_id-500) serving the 14km (8.5 miles) to the city, the bus stop is located by the Departures area, but it's infrequent so most arrivals take a taxi.

Apps

There are several apps that are worth downloading to prepare yourself before you travel to Crete and use during your stay.

Duolingo (https://duolingo.com/) A fun and easy tool to help you brush up on your Greek.

Ferry Hopper (https://ferryhopper.com) A quick and easy way to search, compare and purchase ferry tickets.

Moovit (https://moovitapp.com) shows you public transport with real time information in cities such as Iráklio, Haniá and Rethymno.

Wolt (https://wolt.com) Deliveries of fast food and groceries from local suppliers.

Xe (https://xe.com) Currency conversion and money transfer app.

Bicycle and scooter hire

Bicycle hire: The mountains make long-distance cycling tough work, but in most resorts, you can hire mountain bikes and they'll usually offer good advice on where to explore. Some local travel agents also offer easy bike tours, with a bus to take you up the hills and carry your gear. Crete Bikes (https://cretebike.gr) in Iráklio have electric bikes for hire which is great for getting around the city, while the slightly more adventurous Sports Tours Hellas (https://sportstourshellas.com) in Haniá offer self guided and guided (with professional cyclists) tours around the island.

Scooter hire: Hiring a motorbike is inexpensive – roughly €33 per day in high season for a 50cc machine, or slightly more for a larger engine size. It is illegal to ride a bike of any size without a motorcycle licence. Note that if you ride a motorbike without the right licence, any insurance you have will be void, which could create grave difficulties if you are involved in an accident. Quad bikes, also widely available, are legal to drive with Class B car licenses. Blue Sea, Kosmá Zótou 5-7 (Ikostipémptis Avgoústou) is a reliable Iráklio company that hires scooters and motorbikes (https://bluesearentals.com).

What's the hire charge for a full day? **Póso kostízi giá mía méra?**

Budgeting for your trip

Crete offers good value for money, especially in off-season. But note that prices have increased in recent years. Here are some approximate prices to help you to plan your budget.

Flight from Athens to Iráklio (one way): €80–180 by season

Adult ferry ticket from Athens: €40–117/60–180 (basic seating/cabin)

High-season room in mid-range hotel: €100–120 per night depending on destination

Meal in mid-range taverna: €20–30 per person including basic wine and any tips

Taxi fare from airport to Haniá: Approx €28–30 – but check on arrival

Entrance fee for museums/sites: Range from €5–20. There are sometimes Student and Senior discounts, plus free archaeological site days

Hire (prebooked) of small car (Class A) for two weeks: From €350, but consider hiring a larger category of car, especially if planning to visit mountainous villages

Camping

While free camping (or wild camping) is technically not allowed in Greece, including Crete, it is often tolerated outside of urban areas and tourist centers.

Crete has approximately fifteen official campsites with good facilities such as on-site mini markets, restaurants, shower facilities and free wi-fi.

For camping on the beach, your best bet is Grammeno (https://grammenocamping.gr/en) near Paleochora in Haniá region.

Camping Mithimna (https://campingmithimna.gr/home) is on the northern coast on the way to Elafonisi, again next to the beach and with mountain views.

Car hire

The best car hire rates (under €30 per day) apply to periods of four days or more, with unlimited mileage. Distances on Crete can be considerable, so limited mileage tariffs aren't cost effective. One-way rentals (pick up at one airport, drop off at another) incur surcharges of €35–70.

Reserving before you arrive through an international hire company can be useful, as in peak season demand will be high. Some of the best consolidator websites include https://auto-europe.co.uk; https://carrentals.co.uk; https://rentalcars.com, who also have a downloadable app; and https://rentalcargroup.com. **Alianthos** (https://alianthos-group.com) is an excellent local operator, with offices at airports and major resorts.

You will need a credit card for a damages deposit and a full national licence (held for at least one year) from your country of residence. Non-EU licence holders must, by Greek law, also have an International Driving Permit, except US and UK drivers, where just their national photo driving licence is required. If you fail to provide this, many agencies will refuse to release the car, and if you are caught by the police without it, fines can range upwards of €1000.

Depending on the model and the hire company, the minimum age for hiring a car varies from 21 to 25. Third-party liability insurance and Collision Damage Waiver is usually included in the stated rate, but there is usually a large excess (typically €400–750) before CDW takes effect. One reputable outfit selling such policies is Insurance4CarHire (https://insurance4carhire.com).

Climate

Crete has an average of 320 sunny days per year. Winters are mild, although it can suddenly become cold and wet for short spells. In general, the south coast is hotter, drier and less windy than the north. About 70 percent of the annual rainfall falls between December and March. These are the approximate monthly average temperatures in Iráklio:

		J	F	M	A	M	J	J	A	S	O	N	D
Air (max)	°C	16	16	18	21	24	28	30	39	28	26	21	19
	°F	60	60	64	70	76	82	86	86	82	78	70	66
Air (min)	°C	9	9	10	12	16	18	20	22	20	17	14	11
	°F	48	48	50	54	60	64	68	72	68	62	57	52
Sea	°C	16	16	17	18	20	23	24	25	24	23	19	17
	°F	61	61	63	64	68	73	75	77	75	73	66	63

Crime and safety

Crete is a relatively safe island to visit, with little major crime. However, petty crime and burglaries are on the increase so take precautions: leave valuables in your room safe and don't carry large amounts of cash around. If you are a victim of crime, you will need to contact the local ordinary police (see Police) in the first instance; insurance claims will not be valid without their paperwork.

Driving

Fuel: Fuel in Crete is some of the most expensive in Greece, from around €2 per litre of unleaded 95 in towns, and more in remote areas. Petrol stations are reasonably common, but don't let your tank get too low, especially in the south. Most stations shut by 9pm, and many close on Sunday.
Road conditions: Crete's roads have improved such that now only few parts of the island are inaccessible to a normal hire car. However, most roads have no paved shoulders, which can cause problems if you need to slow and leave the highway. Roads in the interior may be steep with

hairpin turns – always allow extra time even for short distances. You'll often encounter herds of goats and sheep using the roads too. In northern Crete there is a 'motorway' from Agios Nikolaos to Kastelli (Kissamos) via Iráklio, Rethymnon and Haniá, corresponding to a UK dual carriageway. When it is finished, expected to be completed by 2031, the A90, or BOAK, will be Greece's only motorway located on an island, connecting Kissamos with Sitia, a total length of approximately 300km.

Road signs: Signs often come late, hidden by vegetation or not at all, but where they do exist, are mostly international and easily understood, with names in both Roman script and Greek lettering.

Rules and regulations: Greece drives on the right and (theoretically) passes on the left. Yet as with much of the country in general, Cretan drivers observe their own rules; often pulling over with no indicating to talk to friends, double parking, driving on the wrong side of the road, or overtaking in any lane. The largest towns have one-way systems to ease the flow of traffic around the narrow streets, but many motorcyclists (and some car drivers) do not obey these rules. Always expect the unexpected and be aware.

Parking: Although local drivers seem to park where they choose, there are enforced rules. Street parking is permissible, unless stated, but finding a space in towns can be problematic.

Speed limits: 90km/h (56mph) on open roads and 50km/h (30mph) in towns, although most local drivers do not adhere to these limits and have been known to tailgate 'slowcoaches'. Both speed-limit and distance signs are in kilometres. Seat belts are compulsory, as are crash helmets when riding a motorbike – non-observance will net you a draconian fine. Drink-driving laws are strict and control points can test you and pull you off the road instantly. The acceptable alcohol level is 0.05 percent, and 0.02 percent for new drivers and motorcyclists.

Detour **ΠΑΡΑΚΑΨΗ Parákampsi**
Parking **ΠΑΡΚΙΓΚ Párking**
Forbidden **...ΑΠΑΓΟΡΕΥΕΤΑΙ ...apagorévete**

Be careful **ΠΡΟΣΟΧΗ Prosohí**
Stop **ΣΤΑΜΑΤΑ Stamáta**
For pedestrians **ΓΙΑ ΠΕΖΟΥΣ Gia pezoús**
Danger **ΚΙΝΔΙΝΟΣ Kíndinos**
No entry **ΑΠΑΓΟΡΕΥΕΤΑΙ Η ΕΙΣΟΔΟΣ Apagorévete i ísodos**

If you need help: Your car hire office should provide contact numbers for breakdown services. If you are involved in an accident with another vehicle, it is illegal to leave the scene – wait for the ordinary police or traffic police *(trohéa)* to show up and take statements.

Fill the tank please, with (lead-free) petrol **Parakaló, gemíste i dexamení (me amólyvdi)**
My car has broken down **To avtokínito mou éhi halási**

Electricity

The current in Crete is 230v/50Hz. Plugs and outlets are of the European continental two-prong type. Visitors from North America and the UK should bring plug adaptors, as well as dual-voltage shavers and hair dryers if required.

Embassies and consulates

Australian Embassy and Consulate Hatziyianni Mexi Street 5, Level 2, 11528, Athens; 21087 04000; https://greece.embassy.gov.au.

British Vice Consulate Candia Tower, Thalíta 17, Iráklio; 28102 24012; https://bit.ly/UKConsulCrete.

British Embassy and Consulate Ploutárhou 1, 106 75 Athens; 21072 72600; https://gov.uk/world/greece.

Irish Embassy Vassiléos Konstandínou 7, 106 74 Athens; 21072 32771; https://dfa.ie/irish-embassy/greece.

United States Embassy Vassiléos Sofias 91, 115 21 Athens; 21072 12951; https://gr.usembassy.gov.

Emergencies

Important telephone numbers:

General emergency phone number 112 – also used to inform visitors of Emergency Alerts

Police (Emergency) 100

Ambulance (24-hour emergency dispatch) 166

Fire brigade 199

Emergency Alerts Set your phone via Settings/Notifications/Emergency Alerts to receive notifications about any natural danger in your vicinity.

Getting there

By air: Greek airline Aegean (https://aegeanair.com), now incorporating Olympic Airlines, operates daily scheduled flights to Iráklio from Athens, Thessaloniki, Rhodes, and from Athens to Haniá. Sky Express (https://skyexpress.gr) offers flights from many Greek islands to Iráklio, as well as more unusual routes to Sitía. Book well in advance in summer.

Direct scheduled flights from the UK are operated by EasyJet (https://easyjet.com), TUI (https://tui.co.uk), Jet2 (https://jet2.com), British Airways (https://britishairways.com) Ryanair (https://ryanair.com) and Wizz (https://wizzair.com), plus many visitors arrive by charter aircraft. A number of British tour operators offer flight-only or package deals from many UK airports; German, French, Italian and Swiss companies also fly in from around Europe such as Transavia (https://transavia.com) to Haniá and Volotea (https://volotea.com) to Iráklio.

By boat: There are daily car and passenger ferries from Athens (Piraeus) to Iráklio and Haniá, plus two a week between Kíssamos and the Peloponnese. Sailing time varies around 7–9 hours, sometimes longer if overnight. The major companies are Minoan Lines (https://minoan.gr) and ANEK (https://anek.gr). Find up-to-date schedules at https://openseas.gr.

Guides and tours

You can hire a personal, officially licensed guide to accompany you around Knossos, found at the site entrance beyond the ticket office. For guides to other areas, the local tourist office will be able to provide you with details. Many taxi drivers are also happy to act as unofficial guides to their local areas.

Tour companies in every resort offer a variety of day trips by coach or boat, as well as more adventurous jeep safaris in the mountains. You can visit the archeological sites, Samariá Gorge, distant beaches and major towns of Crete from wherever you are staying on the island. One good agency in Haniá is Exploring Creta Tours (https://exploringcreta.com) that offers a plethora of land, sea and mountain tours.

Health and medical care

There are no vaccination requirements for your trip to Crete.

Emergency treatment is given free, although this only covers immediate needs. EU residents can get further free treatment with a European Health Insurance Card (EHIC; available online in Ireland from https://hse.ie). Since Brexit, UK citizens are entitled to free or reduced cost medical treatment on production of a Global Health Insurance Card (GHIC; apply for it online at https://bit.ly/GHICCard). Those in possession of a pre-Brexit EHIC still within its validity date can carry on using it until it expires. Nationals of other countries should check whether their government has a reciprocal health agreement, and/or ensure that they have adequate insurance cover.

It is highly advisable to take out additional travel insurance to cover you for protracted treatment or repatriation.

If you are taking any medication, bring enough for your holiday needs and keep it in its original packaging. If you have a basic medical need, look for a pharmacy, or *farmakío*, signified by a flashing green cross, where you will be able to obtain advice and some medications can be bought over the counter. Most pharmacists speak good English.

Spiny sea urchins can cause serious injury if you step on or graze against them. Avoidance is the best option – they frequent rocky coasts with clean water; wearing swim shoes can help. A more common nuisance are mosquitos, so always use insect repellent in the evenings. Tap water is safe to drink, and indeed, is excellent in the Cretan mountains.

University General Hospital of Iráklio: Leof. Panepistimiou, Iráklio; 28134

02111 (https://pagni.gr/index.php/useful-information).
Ágios Nikólaos: on Knossoú opposite the Archaeological Museum; 28413 43000 (https://agnhosp.gr).
Réthymno: on Triandalídou 19-21; 28313 42100 (https://rethymnohospital.gr).
Haniá: in Mourniés district; 28210 22000 (https://chaniahospital.gr).

a doctor/dentist **énas giatrós/odontogiatrós**
hospital **nosokomío**
an upset stomach **anakatoméno stomáhi**

Language

The sounds of the Greek language do not always correspond to exact equivalents in English, and the letters of the Greek alphabet do not always have a match in the Roman alphabet. This accounts for the divergent spellings of the same place name on Cretan road signs – for example, the word *ágios* is often also spelled *ághios* and *áyios* in the Roman alphabet, although it is always pronounced the same. Emphasis is also a vital element in pronouncing Greek. Throughout this book we have accented vowels within each Greek word to show which syllable to stress. Most people working within the tourist industry will have a basic English vocabulary and many speak English very well.

The table lists the Greek letters in their upper- and lower-case forms, followed by the Roman letters used in this book to transcribe them, and a pronunciation guide.

A	**a**	a	as in *f**a**ther*
B	**β**	v	as in ***v**eto*
Γ	**γ**	g	as in ***g**o* (except before *i* and *e* sounds, when it's like the *y* in ***y**es*)
D	**d**	d	sounds like *th* in ***th**en*

E	**e**	e	as in *get*
Z	**ζ**	z	same as in English
H	**η**	i	as in *ski*
Φ	**θ**	th	as in *thin*
I	**ι**	i	as in *ski*
K	**κ**	k	same as in English
Λ	**λ**	l	same as in English
M	**μ**	m	same as in English
N	**ν**	n	same as in English
Ξ	**ξ**	x	as in *box*
•	**ο**	o	as in *road*
Π	**π**	p	same as in English
P	**ρ**	r	same as in English
Σ	**σ,ς**	s	as in *kiss*, except like *z* before *m* or *g* sounds
T	**τ**	t	same as in English
Y	**υ**	y	as in *country*
Φ	**φ**	f	same as in English
X	**χ**	h	rough, as in Scottish *loch*
Ψ	**ψ**	ps	as in *tipsy*
Ω	**ω**	o	as in *long*
AI	**αι**	e	as in *hay*
AY	**u**	av	as in *avant-garde*
EI	**ει**	i	as in *ski*
EY	**εu**	ev	as in *ever*
OI	**οι**	i	as in *ski*
OY	**ou**	ou	as in *soup*
ΓΓ	**γγ**	ng	as in *longer*
ΓΚ	**γκ**	g	as in *gone*
ΓΞ	**γξ**	nx	as in *anxious*
ΜΠ	**μπ**	b or mb	as in *beg* or *compass*
MS	**ντ**	d or nd	as in *dog* or *under*

LGBTQ+ travellers

Crete is developing its LGBTQ+ scene with Haniá and Iraklíou. Check out cretorama.com/travel-trip-bargain-guides/crete-gay-travel-guide-lgbtq for information of inclusive beaches and LGBTQ+-friendly hotels. Be discreet in the conservative rural communities. Homosexual practice is legal in Greece for people aged over 17 years old.

Money

Currency: The euro (€) is used in Greece. Notes are denominated in 5, 10, 20, 50, 100, 200 and 500 euros; coins in 1 and 2 euros and 1, 2, 5, 10, 20 and 50 cents, known as *leptá* in Greece. Notes of 100 euros and above are regarded with suspicion, as counterfeit, and will often have to be broken down in banks before you can use them.

Currency exchange: Most banks exchange foreign currency but charge a commission (usually 1–3 percent) for the service. Exchange rates appear on a digital display and are generally the same for each bank. You can also change money at bureau de change, found in many tourist centres and open longer hours than banks. Some advertise commission-free transactions, but exchange rates are often inferior to those of banks.

ATMs (cash machines): There are ATMs in every Cretan town or resort of over a few hundred inhabitants. These are the most convenient way to get euros.

Credit cards: Many hotels, restaurants, travel agencies and shops accept credit cards, but there is still a sizeable minority that do not, and out in the countryside credit cards are not generally accepted, especially not AMEX. Contactless payments are becoming more common, although not accepted everywhere, and the maximum amount you can pay without entering a PIN is €50.

Travellers cheques: These are not recommended for use in Greece – expect severe delays or outright refusals in banks or bureaux.

Opening times

Opening times vary between official organisations and privately owned shops and cafés, and also between high and low season. Almost everybody closes mid-afternoon and official entities will not reopen later; if you need to get anything official done, do it in the morning.

Banks are open Monday–Thursday 8am–2.30pm, Fri 8am–2pm. Monday is a typical day of closure for museums, though major attractions will open daily (if perhaps only in the afternoon on Monday).

Shops are generally open Monday, Wednesday and Saturday 9am–2.30pm, closing at 2pm on Tuesday, Thursday and Friday. Note they additionally open from 5.30–8.30pm. Supermarkets open Monday–Friday 9am–9pm, Saturday 9am–4pm; a very few may work Sunday 10am–4pm.

Police

Regular police officers wear two-toned blue uniforms. Tourist police (found in Iráklio, Haniá, Ágios Nikólaos and Hersónisos) also wear blue uniforms displaying a small national flag indicating which language they speak other than Greek. Main police stations are located as follows:

Iráklio: Agiou Artemiou Street 1; 28102 74000.

Ágios Nikólaos: Erythroú Stavroú 47; 28410 91410.

Réthymno: Iroon Politechniou 26; 28310 88100.

Haniá: Iraklíou 23; 28210 25700.

The main website for the Greek police is https://astynomia.gr/?lang=en

Public holidays

Public holidays fall on the following dates:

1 January New Year's Day *(Protohroniá)*

6 January Epiphany *(Theofánia)*

25 March Greek Independence/Annunciation *(Evangelismós)* Day

1 May May Day

15 August Dormition *(Kímisis)* of the Virgin

28 October National *Óhi* ('No') Day

25 December Christmas *(Hristoúgena)*

26 December Gathering of the Virgin's Entourage *(Sýnaxis tis Panagías)*

Moveable dates: The first day of Lent-48 days before Easter (Clean Monday/*Katharí Deftéra*), Good Friday, Easter Monday and Whit Monday/*Agíou Pnévmatos* and Pentecost/*Pentēkostē*

Telephones

The international code for Greece is 30. Within Greece, all landline numbers have ten digits; fixed lines begin with 2, mobiles with 69. Telephone area codes for Crete include: Iraklíou 281, Haniá 282, Rethymno 283 and Lasithi 284.

Since deregulation of the local telecoms market, a number of providers offer competition to the state-run OTE. OTE still, however, maintains most of the increasingly scarce public booths which don't take cash. Yellow kiosks and newsagents sell OTE calling-cards in various unit denomination, as well as other products (including discount long-distance cards and local mobile top-up cards).

Most hotels of two-star rating and above have direct-dial lines, but add a huge surcharge to the cost of calls. Avoid this by using a prepaid, 12-digit-code card with an access number.

Foreign visitors with mobiles can also roam on one of the three Greek networks: Cosmote (https://cosmote.gr), Vodafone (https://vodafone.gr) and Nova (https://nova.gr). For visitors from the UK – since leaving the EU – and other non-EU nationalities, you'll need to check with your provider whether there are roaming fees for using your phone abroad (including texts and data services), or you could go home to a very hefty bill.

If you are staying more than a week or two, it might make sense to buy a local SIM with some talk-time and a data package included. It must be registered at time of purchase, but the number remains valid for a year from each top-up. Make sure your phone is unlocked to accept other SIM cards.

Time zones

Greece is two hours ahead of Greenwich Mean Time and also observes Daylight Savings along with the rest of Europe (but not the USA), moving clocks one hour forward between the last Sunday in March and the last one in October.

In August, here is the time in the following cities:

New York	London	Dublin	Jo'burg	**Crete**	Sydney	Auckland
5am	10am	10am	11am	**noon**	7pm	9pm

Tipping

Service is normally included in restaurant bills, although it is customary to leave between 5 and 10 percent of the bill in small change on the table. It's advisable to leave hotel chambermaids a tip of around €1 per day.

Toilets

Large towns will have public toilets, usually near the marketplace or bus station. Most museums have good public facilities.

Older sewage pipes in Greece are narrower than in most European countries and are easily clogged. It's therefore essential never put toilet paper into the toilet – always use the waste bin provided. Usually there will be a sign in your accommodation reminding you of this. The bin is emptied daily by cleaning staff.

Tourist information

The Greek National Tourist Organisation, or Ellinikós Organismós Tourismoú (EOT; https://visitgreece.gr), is responsible for producing and dispersing tourist information. For information before you travel to Greece, contact one of the following offices:

Australia: 37–49 Pitt Street, Sydney, NSW; (2) 9241 1663.

UK and Ireland: 5th floor east, Great Portland House, 4 Great Portland Street, London, W1W 8QJ, (020) 7495 9300.

US: 305 East 47th Street, New York, NY 10017; (212) 421 5777.

For local tourist information, contact one of the following addresses:

Ágios Nikólaos: Aktí Koundoúrou; 28410 22357.

Haniá: Kydonías 29, inside the city hall; 28213 41665; https://chania tourism.com.

Iráklio: Agiou Titou 1; 2813 409000; https://heraklion.gr.
Réthymno: Delfini Building, Sofoklí Venizélou, town beach; 28310 56350; https://rethymno.gr.

Transport

Buses: An excellent network of affordable bus services crosses the island, with stops at all the major archeological sites. Always arrive slightly ahead of departure time. Tickets are bought on the bus or in advance. Iráklio has two bus stations: on the main road by the ferry port for north-coast services, outside the Haniá Gate for towards Phaistos, Mátala and Agía Galíni. Réthymno bus station is west of the town centre just off the coast road; Haniá's is centrally located on Kydonías, and in Ágios Nikólaos some way out near the Archaeological Museum. For timetables and useful information visit https://rethymnoatcrete.com/bus.htm. The main public bus (KTEL) network site for around Crete is https://e-ktel.com/en.

Taxis: Taxis are numerous, and fares are regulated, but with surcharges for baggage and serving airports. They should have working meters that are set upon departure (to €1.20, not zero; minimum fare €3.20). Agree on hourly or daily rates before you set off.

Boats: Many resort ports are home to seasonal excursion boats, while various south-coast settlements are better connected by scheduled ferry services than by road. The main towns for taking boat trips are Ágios Nikólaos, Agía Galíni, Haniá and Plaka (for Spinalonga island), while daily ferries ply between Hóra Sfakíon, Loutró, Soúgia and Paleóhora.

What's the fare to… ? **Póso éhi éna isitírio giá…?**
When's the next bus to… ? **Póte févgi to epómeno leoforío giá…?**

Visas and entry requirements

European Union (EU) citizens may enter Greece for an unlimited length of time. Citizens of Ireland can enter with a valid identity card or passport. Nationals of the UK, the US, Canada, Australia and New Zealand can stay for up to 90 days within any 180-day period upon production of a valid passport; no advance visas are needed. From the last quarter of 2026, UK citizens will require an ETIAS visa waiver, more information can be found here: bit.ly/ETIASUK. South African citizens require a Schengen Visa, applied for in advance at the nearest Greek embassy or consulate in your home country.

There are no limits on the amount of hard currency visitors can import or export, though amounts in excess of €10,000 equivalent should be declared.

All goods brought into Greece from within the EU must have duty paid on them. There are no limitations on the amount of duty paid goods brought in.

If arriving from a non-EU country (eg Turkey), allowances for duty free goods brought into Greece are as follows: 200 cigarettes or 50 cigars or 250g of tobacco; 1 litre of spirits or 4 litres of wine; 250ml of cologne or 50ml of perfume.

Websites

https://incrediblecrete.com Region of Crete's website on the island's attractions

https://visitgreece.gr Greece's official tourist website

https://explorecrete.com Useful general site with all sorts of info and links

https://climbincrete.com One-stop resource for trekkers and rockclimbers

https://chaniatourism.com Municipality of Haniá's website devoted to tourism

https://heraklion.gr Municipality of Iráklio's website

https://rethymno.gr Official website of Réthymno

https://west-crete.com Labour of love, with plenty of useful links, on all things found west of Réthymno

Another useful source of information is Discover Greece (https://discovergreece.com) – an online platform dedicated to promoting Greek tourism and managed by Marketing Greece.

Index

MINI
CRETE

Second Edition 2026

Editor: Kate Drynan
Author: Rebecca Hall
Picture Editor: Piotr Kala
Picture Manager: Tom Smyth
Cartography Update: Katie Bennett
Layout: Danielle Titmas
Production Operations Manager: Katie Bennett
Publishing Technology Manager: Rebeka Davies
Head of Publishing: Sarah Clark
Photography Credits: Bigstock 26; Britta Jaschinski/Apa Publications 7, 16BL, 40, 96; Georgios Tsichlis/Shutterstock 16BR; iStock 28, 36; Shutterstock 1, 9, 10, 13, 14/15 (all), 16TL 16CL, 18 (all), 20 (all), 23, 25, 30, 32, 34, 38, 43, 45, 46, 49, 50, 53, 54, 56, 58, 61, 62, 65, 69, 70, 72, 74, 76, 79, 81, 82, 84, 87, 89, 90, 92, 94, 99, 101, 102, 105, 106, 108, 110, 112, 115, 116, 121, 122; Yadid Levy/Apa Publications 118
Cover Credits: Knossos Palace **iStock**

About the author
Rebecca Hall's extensive knowledge and deep connection to Greece ensure that her contributions to Rough Guides will be indispensable for first-time visitors and seasoned travelers alike.

Distribution
UK, Ireland and Europe: Apa Publications (UK) Ltd; mail@roughguides.com
United States and Canada: Two Rivers; ips@ingramcontent.com
Australia and New Zealand: Woodslane; info@woodslane.com.au
Worldwide: Apa Publications (UK) Ltd; mail@roughguides.com

Special Sales, Content Licensing and CoPublishing
Rough Guides can be purchased in bulk quantities at discounted prices. We can create special editions, personalized jackets and corporate imprints tailored to your needs.
mail@roughguides.com
roughguides.com

EU Representative
LOGOS EUROPE, 9 rue Nicolas Poussin, 17000, LA ROCHELLE, France; Contact@logoseurope.eu; +33 (0) 667937378

Printed by Omur in Turkey

ISBN: 9781835294086

This book was produced using **Typefi** automated publishing software.

A catalogue record for this book is available from the British Library

Contact us
Every effort has been made to ensure that this publication is accurate, free from safety risks, and provides accurate information. However, changes and errors are inevitable. The publisher is not responsible for any resulting loss, inconvenience, injury or safety concerns arising from the use of this book. If you notice any errors, outdated information, or potential safety risks, please send your comments with the subject line "Rough Guide Mini Crete Update" to mail@roughguides.com.